# Tecumseh and Tenskwatawa: The Lives and Legacies of the Shawnee's Famous Leaders

## By Charles River Editors

**George Catlin's portrait of Tenskwatawa**

# About Charles River Editors

**Charles River Editors** provides superior editing and original writing services across the digital publishing industry, with the expertise to create digital content for publishers across a vast range of subject matter. In addition to providing original digital content for third party publishers, we also republish civilization's greatest literary works, bringing them to new generations of readers via ebooks.

Sign up here to receive updates about free books as we publish them, and visit Our Kindle Author Page to browse today's free promotions and our most recently published Kindle titles.

# Introduction

**A 19<sup>th</sup> century depiction of Tecumseh**

"Brothers, Many winters ago, there was no land; the sun did not rise and set: all was darkness. The Great Spirit made all things. He gave the white people a home beyond the great waters. He supplied these grounds with game, and gave them to his red children; and he gave them strength and courage to defend them." – Tecumseh

Throughout the 19<sup>th</sup> century, American settlers pushing across the Western frontier came into contact with diverse American tribes, producing a series of conflicts ranging from the Great Plains to the Southwest, from the Trail of Tears to the Pacific Northwest. Indian leaders like Geronimo became feared and dreaded men in America, and Sitting Bull's victory over George Custer's 7<sup>th</sup> Cavalry at Little Bighorn was one of the nation's most traumatic military endeavors.

Given this history, Tecumseh's reputation among Americans has been both the most unique and anomalous. As the leader of the Shawnee, Tecumseh was the most famous Native American of the early 19<sup>th</sup> century, and he attempted to peacefully establish a Native American nation east of the Mississippi River in the wake of the American Revolution. While Native Americans, especially in the "Old Northwest" (present-day land west of the Appalachian Mountains and east of the Mississippi River), understood and recognized their own, long established territories and those of other tribes, these boundaries and territories were ignored and unappreciated by the incoming settlers.

As settlers continued to encroach further west, the Shawnee, who were attempting to put together a confederacy of Native Americans to resist, stood firm and ready to fight them. Before America fought Britain in the War of 1812, they were engaged in Tecumseh's War around the Great Lakes. The fighting made him famous and made a military hero (and eventually a president) out of William Henry Harrison, whose victory at Tippecanoe is considered the end of that war.

Despite being one of their most tenacious opponents, Tecumseh almost immediately became a celebrated folk hero and respected leader in American history, all while continuing to be one of the most poignant symbols of resistance among Native Americans. He continues to be a household name across the United States today, nearly 200 years after his death.

What makes Tecumseh's legacy ironic is that the Shawnee were nominally led by a different man altogether, and that man just so happened to be Tecumseh's brother. Lalawethika's early life mostly consisted of abject failures, and he became an alcoholic, but in one of his alcohol-soaked stupors, he began to have visions of the Master of Life that turned him into the Open Door, the prophet named Tenskwatawa. It was Tenskwatawa who brought a new vision to the Shawnee, transforming himself from an object of pity and contempt into a religious leader who had thousands of followers. When the Americans fought at Tippecanoe, the gathering of Native Americans who they were attempting to disperse had congregated at a place colloquially known as Prophetstown.

Tecumseh and Tenskwatawa: The Lives and Legacies of the Shawnee's Famous Leaders

About Charles River Editors

Introduction

## The Origins of the Shawnee

The Shawnee (also, *Shaawanwaki, Šaˑwanoˑki,* and *Shaawanowi lenaweeki*) are an Algonquian-speaking Eastern Woodland Culture native to the eastern forests of North America and linguistically related to the Sauk and Fox peoples. The Shawnee are represented today by three Federally-recognized Shawnee tribes: the Absentee-Shawnee, Eastern Shawnee, and "Loyal" Shawnee (sometimes called the Cherokee Shawnee), all of which are headquartered in Oklahoma. There are also a number of State-recognized tribes and tribes currently petitioning for State recognition in Texas, Missouri, and Kentucky, and several hundred Shawnee live in Canada and Mexico.

In the Algonquian language, "Shawnee" is derived from *shawun* (or *shawunogi*), meaning "southerner", and the name designation is in reference to their original location in the Ohio River Valley relative to other Great Lakes Algonquin groups. In other words, even though the Shawnee live in Oklahoma today, their name has nothing to do with the South, but at least one group did migrate to the Southeast before the reservation era, and they called themselves *Shawano*. Finding the destinations of that group has been complicated due to splitting and frequent migration. That group was called various names, including *Ani-Sawanugi* (Cherokee), *Chaouanons* (French Chauenon), *Chaskpe* (French Chaouesnon), *Chiouanon* (Seneca), *Oshawanoag* (Ottawa), *Satana* (Iroquois), *Shawala* (Lakota), and *Touguenha* (Iroquois). To the colonists of South Carolina, they were known as *Savannah* or *Savannuca*.

The Shawnee historically inhabited the "Ohio Territory" of the Ohio River Valley, which included present-day Ohio, Indiana, part of Pennsylvania, West Virginia, Kentucky, Tennessee, and Michigan. And at one time or another, the Shawnee also occupied Virginia, West Virginia, Western Maryland, South Carolina, Indiana, and Pennsylvania. Given this wide dispersal, they are thought by many historians to have been descendants of the "Fort Ancient" Tradition, a Late Prehistoric cultural tradition of the Ohio River Valley that spanned from 1060-1760. This tradition described groups who settled agricultural villages, are recognized by their shell-tempered pottery, and display a variety of Mississippian style elements. There has also been evidence that the Shawnee may have been in Kentucky, including the discovery of spears and arrow points in vast quantities, but there is little evidence of actual settlement, indicating to historians that Kentucky was most likely a sacred hunting ground rather than an area of settlement.

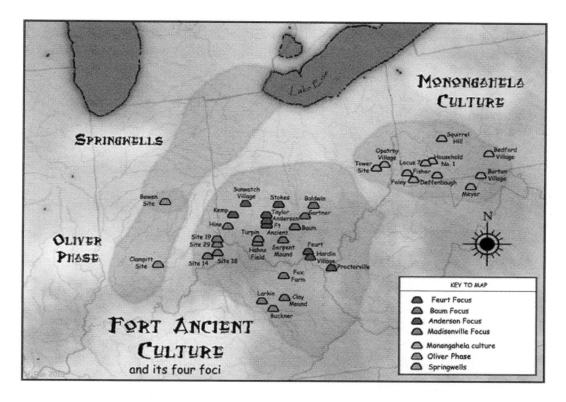

**Map showing the spread of the Fort Ancient culture and Monongahela Culture**

The Shawnee are sometimes confused with the "Pawnee," a Plains group of Oklahoma whose traditional lands were located in northern Kansas and Southern Nebraska, primarily along the Missouri river. The Pawnee, however, are a Caddoan-speaking group whose numbers far exceeded that of the Shawnee, and they were classified a "friendly tribe" by the U. S. Government. The Pawnee have remained primarily in the central United States.

From an archaeological perspective, the Shawnee belong to the Woodland cultural period, a geocultural developmental stage beginning about 2,000-3,000 years ago depending on the scientific criteria and exact physical location. Following the Archaic period from about 1,000-2,000 years ago, the Woodland culture has been found in areas south of the Subarctic and east of the Rocky Mountains, where evidence of widespread agriculture, settled villages, pottery production, and burial mounds are usually present. Variations of the Woodland cultural period have been recognized in the fossil record of the Plains, Midwest, Great Lakes, Northeast, Mid-Atlantic, and U. S. Southeast. It's believed that several groups were part of the Woodland culture, including the Mississippians of the Midwest and Southeast (with whom the Fort Ancient peoples are sometimes associated), the Iroquoians of the Northeast, and the "village-establishing" Plains groups of the Missouri River Valley.

By the time the Shawnee surfaced on the North American landscape as an independent cultural entity, their ancestors had gone through certain developmental stages, including pottery making (with the first pottery of the Upper Ohio River drainage taking place in Ohio about 500 B.C.) and lithic production, with spear/arrow projectile point manufacture advancing through several designs. Early Shawnee pottery was decidedly less ornate than centuries before, small notched and un-notched arrow points were made by the thousands to accommodate use of the bow and arrow, and settlement patterns reflect sustained agriculture, indicating a period of relative regional peace.

It's still unclear which group or groups were the ancestors of the Shawnee, but it's believed to be Algonquin, Fort Ancient, Delaware (whom the Shawnee refer to as their "grandfathers") or the Kickapoo, who by some versions of oral history were once the same tribe as the Shawnee. Additionally, depending on when exactly the Shawnee appeared, they may have initially followed in the footsteps of the Adena moundbuilders, who built hundreds of mound shaped mortuary complexes throughout what would become Shawnee land, but it seems likelier that they arrived later and marveled over these famous earthworks themselves. Either way, by the time the Shawnee migrated into Alabama, the moundbuilding phenomenon became part of their own culture.

**The Serpent Mound in Peebles, Ohio**

Like most Native American groups, Shawnee spirituality reflects the belief that human fortune hinges on the tolerance and patience of the omnipresent spirits who reside in all living things (every fish, animal, and tree) and in every physical place (the earth, water, Sun, Moon, and stars). Since the Shawnee believe it is the interplay of the spirit world that ultimately controls events taking place on the earthly plain, they set aside considerable time to secure their goodwill.

With each new human element added to the Shawnee world, including both other Native Americans and outsiders, the need to respect, appease, and even court the deities became more critical. Thus, by the time of first European contact, numerous ceremonies of thanks and supplication and yearly festivals framed Shawnee life. The "Four Winds," "Earth Mother," and "Corn Woman" were the focus of most observances, and a cycle of rituals evolved. Each spring, several days were devoted to rituals, dances, sporting events, and feasts celebrating the new crops and bounty of the previous winter's hunt, and each fall, the "Festival of Green Corn" acknowledged the bountiful harvest and the people's hopes for continued prosperity. In addition to holding regular purification rituals for Shawnee warriors in the large council house of the village, the Shawnee observed a Bread Dance in the spring when the planting of the fields was completed, the Green Corn Dance to mark the ripening of the crops, and the Bread Dance in the fall as an annual ceremony of thanksgiving. If adversity interrupted this cycle, the village holyman would compose new rituals to appease the spirit world and restore balance.

Integral and inseparable from day-to-day life, every Shawnee represented a spiritual practitioner, if not by profession (as with the holyman and shaman) then by intent. Believing that personal success (whether in procreation, hunting, or longevity) was a matter of obeisance to the spirits, when a Shawnee hunter killed an animal, he performed an impromptu act of thanksgiving to lay the spirit of the animal to rest. Moreover, it was common practice for every Shawnee to occasionally sprinkle tobacco into the campfire as an offering so that the smoke might carry a prayer into the ether. And virtually every Shawnee possessed some sort of fetish he or she manipulated to summon supernatural aid when need be. To the Shawnee, spirituality was all-pervasive, all-encompassing, and all-inclusive.

Central to every Shawnee camp and village were the holymen or shaman, who were among the most respected members of the tribe. The most renowned of these holymen or shaman was Tenskwatawa, the brother of the war chief Tecumseh, and he was known to whites as the "Shawnee Prophet" and at the time considered as important as his brother. From childhood, the Shawnee was taught two fundamental understandings: that holymen were to be held in highest regard for their unique rapport with the spirits, and that they should fear *Weasaloageethee skee.* These were witches (either men or women) who used their spiritual power to influence *Motshee Monetoo*, the "Bad Spirit", who by some reckoning was the counterpart of *Wassshaa Monetoo,* the "Great Spirit" of Shawnee myth. In both oral tradition and myth, witches play prominent roles in the Shawnee worldview.

According to Shawnee cosmology, above all other spiritual entities loomed "The Great Spirit", *Waashaa Monetoo*, who recreated the world after its destruction by flood. *Waashaa Monetoo* had agreed to repopulate the earth at the behest of the only survivor of the Earth's first destruction, the old woman known as *Waupoathee*, who came to be regarded as the Shawnee "Grandmother." *Waupoathee* is said to assist *Waashaa Monetoo* in supervising the Shawnee, making herself visible to those on Earth as the moon.

The Shawnee believed they were the first people *Waashaa Monetoo* created to repopulate the planet and were placed in the center of North America on the banks of the Savannah River, so naturally, the Shawnee believe they hold a special place in the bigger scheme of existence. As the Great Spirit's *special* people, *Waashaa Monetoo* had given the Shawnee a portion of his own heart, as well as a sacred bundle of objects that would help them summon spiritual assistance when in need. Considered the first of the "first-borns," the Mekoche, one of the five primary divisions of Shawnee along with the Hathawekela, Pekowi, Kispoko, and Chillicothe, claimed custody of the tribe's sacred bundle, thereby assuming a predominant and unique status among all the divisions. In 1795, a Mekoche chief was recorded as saying, "The Great Spirit . . . ordered that everything upon the earth should obey us. He put his heart into our tribe and made it the chief of all the tribes. We think we have a right to look upon ourselves as the head tribe of all nations."[1]

Thus, while it has been suggested that ultimately all five Shawnee divisions most likely possessed their own "sacred bundles," the Mekoche were considered superior to the other divisions, along with the Shawnee considering themselves superior to all other peoples. This made for strained relations both within the Shawnee and with neighboring groups. Even so, the inherent spirituality of the Shawnee people is reflected in their familial worldview; they addressed the Delaware as "grandfathers," the Iroquois and Wyandots as "uncles" or "elder brothers," and the Kickapoo as "first brothers". Still, the Shawnee expected other tribes to pay homage to the Shawnee spirits of war, and according to some accounts, even acknowledge the Shawnee spirits as superior to their own.

After suffering the adversities that had resulted in a great reduction in their numbers and their forced dispersal from Ohio to Pennsylvania to Alabama, Shawnee leaders concluded that they had somehow displeased *Waashaa Monetoo,* who they believed had withdrawn his patronage. While some leaders cited the actions of particular individuals, others declared that the tribe had grown corrupt. Still others blamed their misfortune on separation from the Kickapoo, a tribe connected by oral tradition but no living memory of association. Thus, while some cultures' mythology serves as a connection to an ancient past, for the Shawnee of the 18th century, mythological entities were still very much alive and consequential.

Traditional Shawnee social organization was a combination of patrilineal clans, in which individuals trace their most significant kinship relationships through their fathers, and what is known to social scientists as the "Omaha Kinship System," which was based on lineage. Thus, Shawnee children took their clan affiliation from their father, and there were a dozen or more clans symbolized by a different creature of the wild, such as the snake, raccoon, or turkey. Unlike the tribal divisions (Mekoche, Hathawekela, Pekowi, Kispoko, and Chillicothe), clans were exogamous, meaning each clan member was required to choose mates from a clan other

---

[1]  *Sugden, John. Tecumseh: A Life. Page 18.*

than their own. Thus, the clans regulated kinship, with clan affiliation so socially significant that it was incorporated into their personal name. By tradition, clan members believed that through clan affiliation, they derived the powers related to their clan animal.

In his 1871 seminal work *Systems of Consanguinity and Affinity of the Human Family*, socioanthropologist Lewis Henry Morgan identified the Shawnee's "Omaha Kinship System", named for the Omaha people who historically were located in the Northern Plains in present-day Nebraska. This kinship system was patrilineal, with "description" and "classification" of relatives sorted according to descent and gender. The Omaha Kinship System distinguishes between gender and generation, as well as between siblings of opposite sexes in the parental generation, with parallel cousins called brothers and sisters (this system has no equivalent for the English *cousin)*. In the Omaha structure, a distinction is made between cross cousins on the mother's side (children of the mother's brother) and cross cousins on the father's side (children of the father's sister). A mother's brothers' daughters are called *mother*, with mother's brothers' sons called *mother's brother* (or in some settings, *uncle*). Thus, a Shawnee's maternal cross cousins are grouped with individuals in his or her parents' generation. However, for that same Shawnee's paternal cross cousins, the appropriate term depends upon the Shawnee's gender. If he is a male, he calls his father's sisters' children *niece* and *nephew*. If she is a female, she addresses her father's sisters' children as *son* and *daughter*.

Whenever possible, Shawnee settlements were positioned on high ground overlooking the nearby fields where Shawnee women typically laid out and tended their crops. Every village was dominated both conceptually and architecturally by the council house, a large, often fortified building in which all public and ceremonial business was conducted. By and large, most family homes constituted summer shelters only, with village life virtually abandoned in the fall. Erected by the women, the traditional family dwelling was constructed of bark affixed to a framework of wooden posts enclosing a relatively large area of space, and the houses were grouped throughout the village. Many anthropologists assume that some form of societal preference was involved, so that the house arrangement in some regard reflected social status. Sparsely furnished with various platforms serving as seats, tables, and beds, early Europeans described Shawnee houses as well-kept and clean even by their high standards, and reflective of European influence, most houses replaced the traditional smoke hole in the roof with a proper chimney by the 18th century.

During the spring and summer months, Shawnee villages were fully occupied, with most activities revolving around the women, girls, and children. Shawnee children were reportedly allowed almost unlimited freedom while growing up, with the best rewards coming in the form of public praise, and the worse punishment being public shame that had their transgressions announced to friends or visitors. While the men made periodic forays into the wilds to fish and hunt, as well as make or repair weapons and tools as needed, they typically spent most of their time talking amongst themselves, often smoking and gambling for hours on end. Meanwhile, the females tended gardens that produced maize/corn, beans, tobacco, and pumpkins grown in communal fields, collected maple syrup and salt, gathered fruits and medicinal plants, maintained the houses (including making most repairs), and kept the family and communal fires burning. In other words, Shawnee villages had a lively, female-driven community atmosphere, and women were part of a robust system that saw corn become cakes, meat get roasted, and stews and hominy always made available. Women also made clothes and raised children, while somehow still finding time to barter with traders passing through. Summers were social times for family, friends, and visitors alike; one white visitor who visited commonly remarked, "Nothing is too costly or too good to be set before a friend."[2]

In the fall and winter, the larger extended-family groups broke down into smaller core family groups that created individual hunting camps scattered across the "sacred" hunting grounds. During this period, they constructed small, temporary dome-shaped lodges made of wooden poles and animal skins. Serving as their homes until spring, throughout the winter months the women stayed close to base while the men tracked and killed the wild game that provided all their needs. Some historians believe the Shawnee utilized the *atlatl*, a spear-throwing device consisting of a shaft with a cup or spur at one end that supports and propels a dart, during early cultural development, but the majority of physical remains reflect the use of bow & arrow and spear. Of course, after contact with Europeans, the Shawnee quickly adopted firearms for hunting as well.

With the arrival of fall, gender roles were essentially reversed as well. Now it was the men who led their families into the hunting grounds and constructed their winter lodges. While the women tended to all the household needs and rearing of the children, the men provided the game that gave the family not only the meat for sustenance but the bones and pelts for tools, clothing, and trinkets that served as amusement. Years when game was plenty, animal skins were cured and accumulated during the winter to be traded in the spring for such things as muskets, flints, knives, hatchets, kettles, combs, paint, and cloth.

Shawnee numbers were never large. In the mid-1700s, there might have been 1,500 to 2,000 of them in Ohio. Some Shawnee migrated west of their own accord, to escape the continuing wars. Somehow, they maintained a distinct tribal identity during the decades they had been driven out of Ohio.

Conflict intensified just before and during the Revolution. The last British war with the Shawnee was Lord Dunmore's War of 1774. Dunmore, who was the royal governor of Virginia, led a large force into Kentucky and fought a bloody battle at Point Pleasant, which drove the Shawnee back across the Ohio. Between 1775 and 1790, about 80,000 settlers entered Shawnee country, far outnumbering them (Calloway 40, 47).

The Shawnee had been a particularly troublesome people for the U.S. government and settlers

---

[2]  *Harvey, Henry. History of the Shawnee Indians, 1681--1854.*

to deal with. From 1774 to 1794, the Shawnee had been involved in at least 16 armed clashes with Americans. After the defeat of the tribal coalition at the battle of Fallen Timbers in 1794, the tribes had split between those who wanted to accommodate to the Americans and those who wanted to fight. The 1795 Greenville Treaty gave most of Ohio over to settlement, but many Shawnee refused to accept the agreement.

Two of the charismatic Indian leaders who fought in the 1790s, Little Turtle and Blue Jacket, took different routes. Little Turtle took an annuity and accepted the loss of most of Ohio in the Treaty of Greenville. Blue Jacket did not, and settled in an area in northeast Indiana that was still wild and still Indian land. Tecumseh became a follower of Blue Jacket and, in a way, his successor (Smelser 32).

The wars in the Ohio country involved many tribes, not just the Shawnee, but the Shawnee were involved in all of them. In terms of European wars, the battles were just skirmishes, but in terms of all the Indian wars, the wars in the Ohio country were on the same scale as the French and Indian War of 1755-63 and King Philip's War of 1675-78. Thousands of settlers were killed or captured during the wars, and Indian losses, although lower, were severe.

The battles included Point Pleasant in 1774, in which the Virginia colonial militia suffered 75 killed and 140 wounded, but which drove the Shawnee out of Kentucky. There were bloody skirmishes all along the backcountry during the Revolution in which hundreds were killed on both sides. In 1790, the battle known as Harmar's Defeat, led by general Josiah Harmar, cost the lives of more than 180 American soldiers and militia. In 1791, an allied Indian force inflicted the worst defeat ever inflicted by Indians on the American Army, St. Clair's defeat, led by territorial governor Arthur St. Clair, in which 600 soldiers and 200 camp followers were killed, and hundreds more were wounded. In all of these engagements, Indian losses were much lower than those of the militia or Army troops.

In 1794, the American army under Anthony Wayne, a far more capable officer than previous commanders, defeated a large Indian force at the Battle of Fallen Timbers. Wayne's army suffered only about a hundred casualties, but the battle broke the Indian coalition and resulted in the Treaty of Greenville in 1795, which forced the cession of most of the Indian lands remaining in Ohio.

Among the Indian warriors present at Fallen Timbers was a young Shawnee named Tecumseh.

### Tecumseh's Early Years

Tecumseh was born around 1768, on the Mad Creek near Old Piqua, in present-day western Ohio, north of the modern city of Dayton. Popular tradition holds that he was born in "Old Chillicothe," but that village was not founded until 1774. His mother, Methotaske was a Shawnee whose name meant "Lays Eggs in the Sand" or "A turtle laying eggs in the sand," while his father Puckshinwa ("Alights from Flying") was a Muscogee Creek. The two had married while living near present-day Tuscaloosa, Alabama, a result of his mother's Shawnee band having been pushed from the Ohio country by invading Iroquois bands during the 17th century Beaver Wars. When the Shawnee decided to return to the Ohio country, Puckshinwa decided to travel with his wife and was considered a Shawnee because he had married into the tribe.

Like much of Tecumseh's life, his parents' origins are still widely debated. Some historians question who Puckshinwa's ancestors were, with historian John Sugden noting that he "was reputed to have had a British father (presumably a trader)". And there is still debate over whether Methotaske's mother and father were actually Shawnee, because some oral legends claimed she was a Muscogee Creek like Puckshinwa, others asserted she was a Cherokee, and still others claimed she was a white captive.

The literal meaning of Tecumseh's name is described in several different ways, all of which refer to something flying across the sky. Shooting Star ("Tekoomsē" in Shawnee) is one of these translations, but the more widely accepted is Panther Across the Sky ("Tecumtha" or "Tekamthi" in Shawnee). Shooting Star is more descriptive of his period of influence and action, since it was relatively short, while Panther Across the Sky is more descriptive of his action during combat. A British officer (Isaac Brock) and contemporary of the Native American leader would later describe Tecumseh to friends in England saying, "a more sagacious or a gallant warrior does not, I believe, exist."

According to one legend surrounding his name: "As Pucksinwah stared at the sky on this night, he saw a huge meteor streak across from the north, leaving a trail of greenish-white flame. It lasted for fully 20 seconds and was unlike anything he had ever seen before. This was the Panther spirit that the old men sometimes spoke of, and a good sign indeed. As the women around the fire talked excitedly and pointed to the heavens, a baby's cry came from the shelter. Usually a child was not named for several days while the parents waited for a sign to indicate what the great spirit Moneto wished the child to be called, but this child must surely be named Tecumseh, 'The Panther Passing Across'."

Though his son would become the famed fighter, Puckshinwa fought during the French and Indian War, as the Shawnee allied the British against the French. When he was about six years old, Tecumseh's father was killed while fighting in "Lord Dunmore's War" at the Battle of Point Pleasant, on the Ohio River near present-day Point Pleasant, West Virginia.

Learning of his father's death in battle, the young Tecumseh vowed to become a warrior like his father and be like "a fire spreading over the hill and valley, consuming the race of dark souls." When many Shawnee (including his mother) fled west fearing the influx of white settlers, Tecumseh decided to stay behind with his older brother Chiksika and his sister Tecumpease. With both parents gone, Chiksika would raise both Tecumseh and his younger brother

Lalawethika. While Tecumseh would be raised as a warrior, Lalawethika did not have a close relationship with his older brother or sister and thus never learned necessary skills like hunting or fighting.

While Lalawethika was on a far different path that at the time seemed to be leading him to obscurity, Tecumseh followed the path of the warrior, and his first encounter with his erstwhile enemy occurred in 1782 when he joined a Shawnee force that attacked a column of colonial troops invading the Ohio country and led by George Rogers Clark. Tecumseh was panicked by the thunder, violence, and gore of combat and fled from the field of battle. Humiliated and ashamed of himself, he vowed he would never flee from the enemy again.

**The Prophet**

In 1805, a healer among the Shawnee Kishpoko band had a series of intense visions from the Creator, which reformed the life of the man who had them. He declared that the visions offered a new way for the Shawnee and for all the Native Americans.

The healer was an alcoholic shaman named Lalawethika, which has been translated as "The Rattle" and "The Noisemaker." The sense of the names seems to have been something like "loudmouth." He was one of a set of triplets born in 1775, an extremely rare kind of birth, though one of his siblings died as a baby. His mother, Methoataske, was probably Creek, and the father was a Shawnee, Puckeshinwa, who was killed at the Battle of Point Pleasant. Several sources say that Lalawethika was born in 1769, but details of his life vary considerably from source to source.

The family included at least three girls and five boys, one of whom was Tecumseh, born about 1769. Methoataske abandoned the family in 1779, returning to her own people, a group of the Creek nation. The younger children were left in the care of a married older sister, Tecumpeas (Alchetron).

The family did not just lose their father in battle. In 1779, their village was destroyed by raiding Kentucky militiamen, and another village they lived in was destroyed in 1782. An older brother, Chiksika, married a Chicamauga Cherokee woman. He was joined by Tecumseh and a few other Shawnee on a raid, and Chiksika was killed leading it. Tecumseh took over leadership of the small group, and though this may have been Tecumseh's first experience of war, it marked him as a war leader. He returned to Ohio and participated in several of the battles there, including Fallen Timbers (Treuer 100-101).

Lalawethika was not present at the native victories over Harmar or St. Clair, although he was present at Fallen Timbers in 1794 and the Treaty of Greenville in 1795. He appears not to have been much of a warrior, then or later. He joined a community in eastern Indiana Territory, where he fell under the influence of an old medicine man named Penagashea, "Changing Feathers." He tried to apprentice with the old man, who died in 1804, and he learned the basics, including the traditional medicines, medicinal herbs, chants and prayers. He wasn't very successful as a shaman, either. (Edmunds "Tenskwatawa").

Lalawethika's face was marred by his blind right eye. The cause is not clear, but most accounts of his life attribute it to an accident with an arrow somehow damaging his eye. Another account says it was a birth defect. The story about the bow and arrow could be a fabrication designed to make him seem inept at something every Shawnee boy should be able to do, but either way, his blind eye meant that he was unable to hunt, so he necessarily lived on the charity of others. It was also considered something of a physical defect. Lalawethika drowned his sorrows in drink.

Alcohol was the bane of Indian existence and had been since not long after the first European settlements began. Natives wanted iron kettles, textiles, beads, knives, guns and gunpowder, but they also wanted alcohol in whatever form traders made it available, such as gin, whiskey, and cider. They were especially susceptible to alcohol, which led to violence in Indian communities, and some became alcoholics so dependent on drink that they would trade their weapons and the clothes they wore for it.

Lalawethika was a drunk, and in April 1805, he fell into a drunken stupor. The story has it that the stupor was so deep and so long that his family thought he had died and was preparing for his funeral ceremony when he recovered consciousness. When he awoke, he told his family about how he had died and come back to life after receiving visions from the Master of Life and being shown a better way. The tribal peoples traditionally had great respect for visions, and his family and then his village listened with great interest to his account.

After his first visions, Lalawethika gave himself a new name, "Tenskwatawa," usually translated as "Open Door," with the meaning he was the door to access the Master of Life, an entryway to a new future. As he achieved fame and began to accumulate followers, he became known as the Prophet, and to whites as the "Shawnee Prophet."

In his visions, the Creator gave Tenskwatawa detailed instructions for the Indian peoples, and gave him visions of hell, but also of what the earth would look like if the tribes stopped fighting each other and returned to the ways of the ancestors. Shawnee tradition honored a person's visions, and what the Prophet reported of the Creator's wishes was much in the Shawnee tradition and agreeable to his listeners.

In one vision, he saw Indians who sinned by being alcoholics were punished by having molten lead poured down their throats. His initial trance was the last time he used alcohol, so far as is known (Edmunds 265).

Nowhere was the Prophet's new set of rules written down. There was no equivalent of a Tenskwatawa holy book. Many of the details of his prescriptions are known from interactions that followers had with other Indians and with whites, and some whites raised as Shawnee or who were captives provided information. The religion was a whole way of life and its rules were learned orally and retained in memory.

In essence, the Master of Life, the Creator who appeared in Tenskwatawa's visions directed the Indian peoples to unite together and to return to the old ways. When the peoples returned to the old ways and fully divorced themselves from the present, the old world of ample game and ample crops would reappear, and the Americans would be swept away. Repeated visions allowed him to elaborate on the basic themes.

The Prophet's new religion was not just for the Shawnees, as he saw it as the Creator's wish for all the Indian peoples. Indians must stop fighting one another and live in peace. They must, at all costs, avoid alcohol. Ideally, Indians would give up all of the things brought to them by whites, and reject all the clothing, the houses and the foods that originated with the whites. Indians should not eat the meat of creatures the Europeans had brought - pork, beef and mutton. Stone and wood should replace metal. Indians should wear the dress of their ancestors made from the skins and furs of native animals. Gardens should grow the old foods the Creator approved of, which was corn, beans, squash, and potatoes. Men should shave their heads and proudly wear the traditional scalp lock. Property was to be shared in common (Edmonds 267).

The Prophet said that single men must marry, and that wives should obey their husbands, and that men should take only one wife. There is some debate among historians about the rules he posited for husbands and wives. Traditionally, Shawnee women had their own councils that advised the tribal leaders, in effect sharing power, and at least one historian claims that the Prophet's rules eliminated the women's councils, and advocated that husbands beat their wives if they were disobedient (Cave 642).

Tenskwatawa said that Indian women married to white men must leave their husbands and return to their tribe. Mixed race children were to stay with their fathers. Christian Indians must abandon their faith because it was associated with the Americans (Edmunds "Tenskwatawa").

Shawnee tradition held that their ancestors had crossed a great water to find their home. On the way, they had to kill a great water serpent that was the source of evil in the universe. The traditions held also that malevolent witches and their witchcraft was responsible for problems (Edmunds 261).

Tenskwatawa was a shaman very much in the Shawnee tradition, but he had no hesitation in defying that tradition if he thought it was in accordance with what his visions indicated the Creator wished. It was traditional for Shawnee shamans to have what has been described as a medicine bundle, with odds and ends of things such as eagle feathers, sacred to that person, that were thought to offer the possessor protection and spiritual power. The Prophet ordered Indians to do away with their medicine bundles, because, he said, they were used by witches. He substituted prayer sticks, literal sticks that had symbols carved into them, intended to remind the people to pray to the Creator both at morning and in the evening (Cave 643).

Tenskwatawa told his followers that the Master of Life had created Indians, the Spanish, French and the British, but that Americans had come from the scum of the great water. In Shawnee tradition, that would mean that Americans were created by the forces of evil. The Creator hated the Americans, he said, because although the Americans were numerous, they were unjust and took the land that the Creator had designated for the Shawnee and for the Indian peoples. Indians should distance themselves from Americans if they could, and avoid shaking their hands. For Tenskwatawa, Americans were, by their nature, the embodiment of evil (Edmonds 268).

Adherents to the new religion must always support the infirm and the old, and help others. They should share game they killed with the hungry. Animal skins must not be harvested for sale for money, but offered for things that people needed. The Prophet said that the Creator disliked the fur trade and the cash economy of buying and selling things. The return to the old ways offered a better future, one devoid of Americans. Once the Indian peoples began to obey, the Great Spirit would return game to the woods, and bows and arrows would be sufficient to hunt for the people to be fed, and they would no longer need guns and gunpowder (Cave 642).

His followers banded together and created a town of adherents at Greenville, in northwest Ohio, an area still largely free from American settlers, although it was the location where the Greenville Treaty had been forced on the Indians. The group was sizable for an Indian town, perhaps 200 Kishpokos and Pekowis and a hundred or more others. The settlement kept growing as the number of the Prophet's followers grew. The settlement was on the U.S. side of the boundary that had resulted from the 1795 Treaty of Greenville, which displeased the state authorities - Ohio became a state in 1803 (Lakomaki 616).

At Greenville, and later at Prophetstown on the Tippecanoe River, the settlement built several large structures, including a council lodge, and a place called the House of the Stranger for visitors, who would most often be pilgrims coming to hear Tenskwatawa's message (Poling 36).

An incident involving Governor William Henry Harrison that greatly strengthened the Prophet's credibility with all the Indian groups came when Harrison wrote to a group of Delawares. Harrison wanted to discredit the Prophet and expose him as a charlatan. The letter that Harrison sent to the Delaware council said they should demand proof from Tenskwatawa that he was a real messenger from God, and that they should demand that he perform a miracle. Harrison said that they should "ask him to cause the sun to stand still, cause the moon to alter its course, the rivers to cease to flow, or the dead to rise from their graves."

**Harrison**

Tenskwatawa learned of the letter and complied with Harrison's request for a miracle by stopping the sun on June 16, 1806. He had predicted a solar eclipse, announcing it to his followers some weeks before the solar eclipse occurred. His followers were stunned, and news of the miracle he performed spread like wildfire, hugely enhancing his status as the voice of the Creator.

It seems unlikely that Tenskwatawa or his brother had the math skills or the astronomical knowhow to predict the eclipse. It might have been just a lucky prediction, and others speculate that Tecumseh had read about it in some edition of a farmer's almanac, a common genre at the time. Such an almanac would have had an assortment of information, including lists of coming eclipses. Tecumseh was known to be an able speaker of several languages, and he may have tried learning to read English and learned of the coming eclipse that way. Perhaps one of the brothers learned of it from a schoolteacher or missionary. Whatever the source of the information, the Prophet's legitimacy was cemented by appearing before his followers and predicting the eclipse (Kramer).

Tenskwatawa did not have just one set of visions. He continued to have visions and to hear what the Creator wished for the people. Stephen Ruddell was a white captive brought up as a

Shawnee. Later in his life, he wrote about how the Prophet would ritually purify himself and then enter a dark wigwam, clothed in wildcat skins, wearing the shoulder blades of a deer, and then chant for days in the darkness inside. Ruddell was not a convert, but he seems to have admired the Prophet's sanctity and concerns for the people, and Ruddell found the Prophet to be sincere and impressive (Cave 643).

The Prophet and his views were known quite widely. President Thomas Jefferson mentioned Tenskwatawa in a letter to John Adams, calling him "the Wabash Prophet," and doubting the legitimacy of his message. Jefferson characterized him as "more rogue than fool," and plainly considered him to be a charlatan for credulous believers (Andrews 115).

Jefferson probably heard about the Prophet from reports by Harrison, who Jefferson had appointed governor of Indiana Territory. Jefferson's own attitude about religion was notably skeptical, and he literally cut and pasted the New Testament into a volume of Jesus' sayings, leaving out almost all the religion and turning it into a book of philosophy, which has come to be named "The Jefferson Bible." It's no wonder that he characterized Tenskwatawa as a "rogue," given Jefferson's apparent skepticism of religious figures.

The Prophet's settlement at Greenville, sometimes confusingly also called Prophetstown, was open and hospitable to visitors. In 1807, several Shakers in a mission to the Shawnees visited Greenville and stayed for several days. They wrote a long report about their visit, their conversations with various Indian residents of Greenville, and their impressions from seeing Tenskwatawa preach to his followers. The Prophet did not speak English, so the Shaker mission relied on a translator, which means they may or may not have gotten honest translations. Indian translators were sometimes known to "translate" into words that the listeners wanted to hear, rather than what was really said.

The Shakers themselves were the followers of a prophet who had messages from the Creator and who was viewed with hostility by both British and Americans. Mother Ann Lee brought her visions to the colonies and developed the Shaker way in the years during and following the Revolution. There were far more Shakers than there were Shawnees. Like the Shakers who had no problems with taking in believers, regardless of social status, the Prophet's community was open to believers from any tribe.

The Shakers were impressed with Tenskwatawa's view that alcohol was evil, and they were sympathetic with his views that Indians should return to the old ways and live separate from whites. The Shaker way was also a kind of withdrawal from the world into colonies of believers. They had begun to set up a colony near Vincennes.

This 1807 Shaker mission's report described watching Tenskwatawa speak to a group of about 25 men, some of them visitors from another tribe. They describe the Prophet as a man of serious bearing with an impressive and dignified way of speaking. They were impressed with the cleanliness and orderliness of Greenville and thought it not unlike a Shaker colony (Andrews 120).

Greenville would have been unlike a Shaker colony in the sense that the Shakers lived in collective dormitories with rigid separation between the sexes, while, in Greenville, people continued to live in families. The Shakers also welcomed visitors and let them watch worship services, like the Prophet's Greenville did. The Shaker services involved dancing, and the Shawnee seem to have adapted traditional dances to the Prophet's vision.

The visiting Shakers described a large building that was dedicated to religion. They described it as plain, solemn and godly. They wrote in their report that they were pleased to find "such a work of God among a noble and likely and resolute people" (Andrews 126).

The Shakers probably noted some similarities, including a religious community set among an unfriendly neighborhood of not always tolerant Christians. They also would have been more sympathetic than most Americans to the Prophet's claims to have had conversations with God, because the Shaker founder, Mother Lee, had reported similar visions.

The Shakers in Indiana, like the Shakers elsewhere, performed a variety of services for their neighbors for small fees, and sometimes out of neighborliness. They provided blacksmith work such as repairing and sharpening tools. They did so for Indians, until governor Harrison issued an order against "smith work" being done for the Indians, claiming that sharpening tools was really sharpening weapons (Andrews 115).

As word of the Prophet's visions spread, the numbers of his followers increased. Groups from other bands visited Prophetstown, sometimes traveling hundreds of miles. Among the tribes the visitors came from were Ottawas, Chippewas, Winnebagoes, Menominees, and Potawatomies. Some of the visitors stayed in the town, and some returned home. Some of those returning home were converts to the Prophet's new religion, but it is not known how wide their influence might have been. There were no satellite towns growing up elsewhere, and there was no equivalent of a clergy or missionaries, but enthusiasts spread the word all over the Great Lakes region (Edmonds 270).

Tenskwatawa disliked people he thought were witches. In what is perhaps the most dislikable aspect of his visionary revival, he participated in at least one active witch hunt. In an 1806 visit to Woapikamunk, a Delaware village in Ohio, he was anxious about what he felt was the malevolence of practicing witches.

The village residents assembled, and after praying for guidance, the Prophet pointed out five people as witches. One was a woman raised by Moravian missionaries, the second was a chief who advocated co-operation with the Americans, and the third was a man who had been an interpreter for the Moravians. The fourth was a convert to Christianity, and the fifth was the wife of a chief also accused of working with the Americans. The first four were executed by burning at the stake, and the fifth somehow avoided execution. These are the only known witches whose executions the Prophet actually ordered (Bell 61).

This severe witch hunt aroused fierce opposition among the Delaware tribe and among other Indian groups. Traditionally, witches had been persecuted by many Indian peoples, but Tenskwatawa's going through a village and seeking out witches proved to be too much, and he did not do it again. It is not known if his followers elsewhere hunted down alleged witches.

The Prophet's number of followers grew, and in 1808 they decided to move to more hospitable grounds, without the hostility they faced in Greenville. Some Shawnee did not credit the Prophet's vision, and the ever-increasing number of settlers were deeply suspicious of the growing numbers of Indians at Greenville. They were invited, apparently reluctantly, to settle in what is now Indiana, at a spot near where the Tippecanoe River flows into the Wabash. The area was recognized as belonging to the Miami tribe, which had been hospitable to Shawnees in the past. The Miamis had been in the region for many years, controlling the canoe portage from the north-flowing Maumee River to the south-flowing Wabash.

The Treaty of Greenville had turned over most of Ohio to settlement. The problem with the treaty was the same as most other treaties like it. The Indian peoples were supposed to observe it, but settlers usually ignored it. Frontier whites routinely crossed into Indian land to hunt and to settle. Any Indian who ventured near a squatter settlement risked being shot. In 1801, Harrison observed that frontiersman "consider the murder of Indians in the highest degree meritorious" (Edmunds "Justice" 48).

Word of the Prophet's overall message reached the Americans, and the British in Canada. The Americans generally seem to have thought that it was somehow a British plot. No one had forgotten the powerful Indian confederacy created a generation before by the Ottawa chief Pontiac combining the preaching of the prophet Neolin with a message of unity and resistance.

Called "Pontiac's Rebellion," the 1763-1765 war nearly succeeded in driving the British out of the Great Lakes region. The war ended in a kind of draw, with the British and Pontiac agreeing to end hostilities. The huge expense of the war led to the British policy of reserving the land from the crest of the Appalachians to the Mississippi for the tribes. The British issued an order forbidding settlers from crossing the Appalachians and taking Indian lands. That order was one of the main causes of the colonists revolting against British rule.

The war chief Pontiac, and the prophet Neolin, were a combination that resulted in a formidable Indian resistance. Neolin was a member of the Delaware people in Ohio, and was sometimes called "The Delaware Prophet." Neolin preached that the ways of the white people had corrupted the Indians, and that a complete separation must occur. Pontiac used Neolin's preaching to help create his confederacy. The combination of the Prophet and his formidable brother Tecumseh must have been a worrisome parallel with memories of that earlier resistance. Whether Tenskwatawa had any connection with any surviving followers of Neolin is not known, but seems likely.

The population of Prophetstown increased to an almost unsupportable level. The population rose to about 3,000 at its peak, huge for an Indian settlement, and very difficult to provision. Game, such as deer, became more and more scarce, and they had grown an insufficient amount of corn squash and beans to feed all the pilgrims. During the winters of 1808-09 and 1809-10, residents faced severe problems and, in the winter of 1809-10, some of the residents starved to death. The British sent some supplies after Indians from the town visited Amherstburg, the British center just over the border in Canada, and pleaded for help.

The winter hunger does not seem to have dulled his followers' enthusiasm for the Prophet's message, though not all the residents of Prophetstown shared in Tenskwatawa's vision. An occasional resident of Prophetstown was the Potawatomie chief, Main Poc, who was powerful enough to defy the rules. He continued to deal in alcohol, he resented the prohibition on trading with the Americans, and parties of his group's warriors raided white settlements in Illinois and raided the Osages, as well. Main Poc considered himself not bound by the Prophet's declaration of peace and separation (Bottinger "Prophet" 39).

To rid the country of whites and restore Indians to their lost territories and former ways of life, Tenskwatawa seems to have been depending upon faith in the Great Spirit and some kind of apocalyptic event. For his part, Tecumseh, whether he was a true believer or not in his brother's teachings, followed a more reality-based approach. Tecumseh spent a good bit of his time away from Prophetstown visiting with other Indians and urging them to unify against further cessions of Indian lands.

### The Confederacy

After Fallen Timbers, many Native American leaders were giving up the fight, but Tecumseh did not agree with the conditions of the treaty and was not among the Native American leaders who signed the treaty. By all accounts, the scared 14 year old boy who had run from the field of battle had been very efficiently and effectively trained in the Native American art of warfare by his brother Chiksika. Tecumseh's experience in both small and large-scale military conflicts against settlers and the U.S. military had taught him to judiciously deploy military assets.

Moreover, Tecumseh had grown into a skilled and charismatic orator, a vital skill that he would use to help build a new confederacy of Native American tribes that he hoped would extend from the Great Lakes to the Gulf of Mexico and form a barrier against further encroachment by white settlers. Unlike other Shawnee and Northwest Native American leaders, Tecumseh advocated violent resistance to white settlement, and this attitude appealed greatly to younger warriors who sought prestige through combat.

In the summer of 1809, Tecumseh took the message of unity to the Indians in Ohio, the first of what would be a series of outreach travels covering thousands of miles. Tecumseh traveled around the lower Great Lakes region that year, visiting Native American leaders and using his considerable rhetorical and oratorical skills to urge them to stop cooperating with invading Americans and threatening to kill those leaders who continued to do so. As his best biographer, John Sugden, put it, the Treaty of Fort Wayne on September 30, 1809 was "a treaty too far" for Tecumseh. Signed by chiefs of the Delaware, Potawatomi, Miami and Eel River tribes, the treaty ceded a large territory north of Vincennes to the U.S. government. When some of the Miamis were reluctant at first to sign, Harrison put aside his previously avowed scruples about mixing up Indians with liquor and served some of it to them on this occasion. Tecumseh was outraged that the chiefs, including the former Miami resistance leader Little Turtle, had been bribed into giving up 3 million more acres of land. Tecumseh now felt that all the treaties made since the Treaty of Greenville were invalid, and that the natives should refuse the annuities. If older chiefs had become corrupted by annuities, then younger warriors should push them aside and take over power. In fact, after the signing of the Treaty of Fort Wayne in 1809, Tecumseh warned Native American leaders who had signed the treaty that those who attempted to carry out the terms would be killed.

The real goal for Tecumseh was to convince Native Americans to unite in a multi-tribal confederacy strong enough to halt westward expansion by settlers. Numerous tribal leaders agreed to join Tecumseh's confederacy, but even those who did not lost warriors and families to the Prophetstown settlement. It's believed that in 1808, Tecumseh had about 5,000 warriors at his disposal, scattered about the region in villages or at Prophetstown, and that same year the British in Canada approached the leader hoping to form an alliance. The British and U.S. had seen their own tensions rise over issues like trade and the British impressments of American sailors, and they would fight the War of 1812 a few years later. At this time, however, Tecumseh refused the offer and gradually grew to become the leader of the confederacy, much of which was built upon the religious appeal of his brother's purification movement.

**Tippecanoe**

As fate would have it, the main white leader in the years before the Battle of Tippecanoe in 1811 was William Henry Harrison. Although a legend later grew up about his humble log cabin origins, Harrison, born in 1773, was actually the scion of an old Virginia slave plantation family, and his father was one of the signers of the Declaration of Independence. At the age of 18, Harrison joined the U.S. Army, and he served as "Mad Anthony" Wayne's aide de camp at the Battle of Fallen Timbers and during the negotiations that led to the Treaty of Greenville (of which he was one of the signers).

After resigning from the Army, he quickly rose through the political ranks of the Northwest Territory, from his appointment as its Secretary to serving as its first elected delegate to

Congress. In 1800, at just 27 years old, he became the Governor of the newly-created Indiana Territory when the Northwest was split into Ohio and it. He has been referred to as the "George Washington" of the Northwest.

Harrison was not without sympathy for the plight of the Indians. In a letter to the Secretary of War in 1801, he wrote, "For the last ten or twelve weeks I have been constantly engaged in receiving visits from the Chiefs of most of the Indian nations which inhabit this part of the Territory. They all profess and I believe that most of them feel a friendship for the United States—but they make heavy complaints of ill treatment on the part of our Citizens. They say that their people have been killed—their lands settled on—their game wontonly destroyed—& their young men made drunk & cheated of the peltries which formerly procured them necessary articles of Clothing, arms and ammunition to hunt with. Of the truth of all these charges I am well convinced." Harrison, in this letter, went on to detail the unpunished murders of Indians by frontiersmen, who often thought of killing an Indian as a "meritorious act," and he described the heedless slaughter by whites of animals necessary for the natives' subsistence.

By 1810, the United States had noticed Tecumseh's influence and had become concerned about the Native Americans' organization, not to mention their increasingly militant attitude. Since his appointment as Indiana governor in 1800, Harrison had been working to attract sufficient white settlers into the Indiana Territory to begin a petition for statehood, and he had steadily managed to cede territory from Native American to United States ownership. Meanwhile, Tecumseh had continued traveling and recruiting other Native American groups, reviving the idea of a pan-tribal ownership of Native American territory that had been advocated earlier by Mohawk Chief Joseph Brant and Shawnee Chief Blue Jacket.

One of the seminal and most legendary moments of the era took place in 1810 when Tecumseh and about 400 warriors marched to Governor Harrison's house to meet with Harrison, where they demanded that the Treaty of Fort Wayne be rescinded and that American settlers should not try to begin settling the newly acquired territory. With his warriors dressed up and wearing war paint, Tecumseh and the group unnerved the townspeople at Vincennes, but Harrison kept calm, even as the situation seemed about to deteriorate. Harrison denied any need to nullify the Fort Wayne treaty and dismissed Tecumseh's ideas regarding Native American land ownership, insisting that the United States could deal with tribes individually and that if the Indians were truly one nation they'd all speak one language. In response, Tecumseh became more agitated and said to the governor, "You have the liberty to return to your own country ... you wish to prevent the Indians from doing as we wish them, to unite and let them consider their lands as common property of the whole ... You never see an Indian endeavor to make the white people do this ... Sell a country! Why not sell the air, the great sea, as well as the earth? Did not the Great Spirit make them all for the use of his children? How can we have confidence in the white people?"

**Grouseland (Harrison's house)**

Since Tecumseh was speaking a language Harrison was unable to understand, at this point one Shawnee working with Harrison and the settlers signaled that Tecumseh appeared to be whipping up his group and possibly intended to kill Harrison. As that Shawnee cocked his pistol, Harrison pulled out his sword, and the garrison defending the town added to the stand-off. Seeking to ensure cooler heads prevailed, Potawatomi Chief Winnemac urged Tecumseh and the warriors to leave peacefully, and as they left Tecumseh told Harrison he would ally with the British unless the Treaty of Fort Wayne was rescinded.

**A depiction of the famous encounter between Tecumseh and Harrison**

Tecumseh met again with Harrison in August 1811 at the latter's home in Vincennes after Harrison summoned him to answer for the murder of some settlers. Tecumseh assured the governor that he and his Native American brothers at Prophetstown intended to maintain peace with the United States, but that there were still differences between the two sides that had to be bridged. With nothing being settled at the meeting in 1811, both sides could sense war was looming on the horizon.

Tecumseh was now convinced "the only way to stop this evil is for the red man to unite in claiming a common and equal right in the land, as it was first, and should be now, for it was never divided." Thus, after his August meeting with Harrison, Tecumseh left his brother Tenskwatawa in command of his confederate allies and traveled south, eventually meeting with each of the "Five Civilized Tribes". The Cherokee, Choctaw, Muscogee, Chickasaw, and Seminole were so-named because European American settlers considered them civilized as a result of the fact they had largely adopted colonial ways. These tribes were all descended from the Mississippian Culture that developed planned, quasi-urban towns (often of several thousand people), engaged in organized agriculture of corn and beans, and appointed religious and political leaders hereditarily. Commonly called "the Mound Builders," The Mississippian

Culture existed in a series of matriarchal villages throughout the Midwest, Eastern, and Southeastern present-day United States between 800 and 1500 A.D., comprised of Native American cultures as complex and vibrant as the Aztec and Maya civilizations of Mesoamerica. These so-called civilized tribes were in fact descendants of their own complex and indigenous civilization.

One of Tecumseh's most famous speeches was given before a joint council of the Choctaw and Chickasaw nations. Titled "Sleep Not Longer O Choctaws and Chickasaws", Tecumseh attempted to convince them of the impending danger and the need to band together to resist the settlers:

"In view of questions of vast importance, have we met together in solemn council tonight. Nor should we here debate whether we have been wronged and injured, but by what measures we should avenge ourselves; for our merciless oppressors, having long since planned out their proceedings, are not about to make, but have and are still making attacks upon our race who have as yet come to no resolution. Nor are we ignorant by what steps, and by what gradual advances, the whites break in upon our neighbors. Imagining themselves to be still undiscovered, they show themselves the less audacious because you are insensible. The whites are already nearly a match for us all united, and too strong for any one tribe alone to resist; so that unless we support one another with our collective and united forces; unless every tribe unanimously combines to give check to the ambition and avarice of the whites, they will soon conquer us apart and disunited, and we will be driven away from our native country and scattered as autumnal leaves before the wind.

"But have we not courage enough remaining to defend our country and maintain our ancient independence? Will we calmly suffer the white intruders and tyrants to enslave us? Shall it be said of our race that we knew not how to extricate ourselves from the three most dreadful calamities — folly, inactivity and cowardice? But what need is there to speak of the past? It speaks for itself and asks, Where today is the Pequod? Where the Narragansetts, the Mohawks, Pocanokets, and many other once powerful tribes of our race? They have vanished before the avarice and oppression of the white men, as snow before a summer sun. In the vain hope of alone defending their ancient possessions, they have fallen in the wars with the white men. Look abroad over their once beautiful country, and what see you now? Naught but the ravages of the paleface destroyers meet our eyes. So it will be with you Choctaws and Chickasaws! Soon your mighty forest trees, under the shade of whose wide spreading branches you have played in infancy, sported in boyhood, and now rest your wearied limbs after the fatigue of the chase, will be cut down to fence in the land which the white intruders dare to call their own. Soon their broad roads will pass over the grave of your fathers, and the place of their rest will be blotted out forever. The annihilation of our race is at hand unless we unite in one common cause against the common foe. Think not, brave Choctaws and Chickasaws, that you can remain passive and indifferent to the common danger, and thus escape the common fate. Your people, too, will soon be as falling leaves and scattering clouds before their blighting breath. You, too, will be driven away from your native land and ancient domains as leaves are driven before the wintry storms.

"Sleep not longer, O Choctaws and Chickasaws, in false security and delusive hopes. Our broad domains are fast escaping from our grasp. Every year our white intruders become more greedy, exacting, oppressive and overbearing. Every year contentions spring up between them and our people and when blood is shed we have to make atonement whether right or wrong, at the cost of the lives of our greatest chiefs, and the yielding up of large tracts of our lands. Before the palefaces came among us, we enjoyed the happiness of unbounded freedom, and were acquainted with neither riches, wants nor oppression. How is it now? Wants and oppression are our lot; for are we not controlled in everything, and dare we move without asking, by your leave? Are we not being stripped day by day of the little that remains of our ancient liberty? Do they not even kick and strike us as they do their blackfaces? How long will it be before they will tie us to a post and whip us, and make us work for them in their cornfields as they do them? Shall we wait for that moment or shall we die fighting before submitting to such ignominy?

"Have we not for years had before our eyes a sample of their designs, and are they not sufficient harbingers of their future determinations? Will we not soon be driven from our respective countries and the graves of our ancestors? Will not the bones of our dead be plowed up, and their graves be turned into fields? Shall we calmly wait until they become so numerous that we will no longer be able to resist oppression? Will we wait to be destroyed in our turn, without making an effort worthy of our race? Shall we give up our homes, our country, bequeathed to us by the Great Spirit, the graves of our dead, and everything that is dear and sacred to us, without a struggle? I know you will cry with me: Never! Never! Then let us by unity of action destroy them all, which we now can do, or drive them back whence they came. War or extermination is now our only choice. Which do you choose? I know your answer. Therefore, I now call on you, brave Choctaws and Chickasaws, to assist in the just cause of liberating our race from the grasp of our faithless invaders and heartless oppressors. The white usurpation in our common country must be stopped, or we, its rightful owners, be forever destroyed and wiped out as a race of people. I am now at the head of many warriors backed by the strong arm of English soldiers. Choctaws and Chickasaws, you have too long borne with grievous usurpation inflicted by the arrogant Americans. Be no longer their dupes. If there be one here tonight who believes that his rights will not sooner or later be taken from him by the avaricious American pale-faces, his ignorance ought to excite pity, for he knows little of the character of our common foe.

"And if there be one among you mad enough to undervalue the growing power of the white race among us, let him tremble in considering the fearful woes he will bring down upon our entire race, if by his criminal indifference he assists the designs of our common enemy against our common country. Then listen to the voice of duty, of honor, of nature and of your endangered country. Let us form one body, one heart, and defend to the last warrior our country, our homes, our liberty, and the graves of our fathers.

"Choctaws and Chickasaws, you are among the few of our race who sit indolently at ease. You have indeed enjoyed the reputation of being brave, but will you be indebted for it more from report than fact? Will you let the whites encroach upon your domains even to your very door before you will assert your rights in resistance? Let no one in this council imagine that I speak more from malice against the paleface Americans than just grounds of complaint. Complaint is just toward friends who have failed in their duty; accusation is against enemies guilty of injustice. And surely, if any people ever had, we have good and just reasons to believe we have ample grounds to accuse the Americans of injustice; especially when such great acts of injustice have been committed by them upon our race, of which they seem to have no manner of regard, or even to reflect. They are a people fond of innovations, quick to contrive and quick to put their schemes into effectual execution no matter how great the wrong and injury to us; while we are content to preserve what we already have. Their designs are to enlarge their possessions by taking yours in turn; and will you, can you longer dally, O Choctaws and Chickasaws?

"Do you imagine that that people will not continue longest in the enjoyment of peace who timely prepare to vindicate themselves, and manifest a determined resolution to do themselves right whenever they are wronged? Far otherwise. Then haste to the relief of our common cause, as by consanguinity of blood you are bound; lest the day be not far distant when you will be left single-handed and alone to the cruel mercy of our most inveterate foe."

As he tried to find allies among the Five Civilized Tribes, Tecumseh also gave an impassioned war speech in October 1811 during a meeting with the Muscogee Creek, the tribe his father was believed to have belonged to: "In defiance of the white warriors of Ohio and Kentucky, I have traveled through their settlements, once our favorite hunting grounds. No war-whoop was sounded, but there is blood on our knives. The Pale-faces felt the blow, but knew not whence it came. Accursed be the race that has seized on our country and made women of our warriors. Our fathers, from their tombs, reproach us as slaves and cowards. I hear them now in the wailing winds. The Muscogee was once a mighty people. The Georgians trembled at your war-whoop, and the maidens of my tribe, on the distant lakes, sung the prowess of your warriors and sighed for their embraces. Now your very blood is white; your tomahawks have no edge; your bows and arrows were buried with your fathers. Oh! Muscogees, brethren of my mother, brush from your eyelids the sleep of slavery; once more strike for vengeance; once more for your country. The spirits of the mighty dead complain. Their tears drop from the weeping skies. Let the white race perish. They seize your land; they corrupt your women; they trample on the ashes of your dead! Back, whence they came, upon a trail of blood, they must be driven. Back! back, ay, into the great water whose accursed waves brought them to our shores! Burn their dwellings! Destroy their stock! Slay their wives and children! The Red Man owns the country, and the Pale-faces must never enjoy it. War now! War forever! War upon the living! War upon the dead! Dig their very corpses from the grave. Our country must give no rest to a white man's bones. This is the will of the Great Spirit, revealed to my brother, his familiar, the Prophet of the Lakes. He sends me to you. All the tribes of the north are dancing the war-dance. Two mighty warriors across the seas will send us arms. Tecumseh will soon return to his country. My prophets shall tarry with you. They will stand between you and the bullets of your enemies. When the white men approach you the yawning earth shall swallow them up. Soon shall you see my arm of fire stretched athwart the sky. I will stamp my foot at Tippecanoe, and the very earth shall shake."

Despite Tecumseh's pleas, most of the southern tribes refused Tecumseh's offers. Choctaw Chief Pushmataha countered Tecumseh by claiming coexistence was possible and advocated abiding by the terms of the treaties: "These white Americans ... give us fair exchange, their cloth, their guns, their tools, implements, and other things which the Choctaws need but do not make ... So in marked contrast with the experience of the Shawnee, it will be seen that the whites and Indians in this section are living on friendly and mutually beneficial terms."

# Portrait of Pushmataha

Only a faction (Upper Creek) of the Creek Nation, called the Red Sticks, responded to Tecumseh's call for violent resistance. Like Tecumseh, the Red Sticks had seen their brethren among the Lower Creek make land cessions in their ancestral homelands (modern Georgia) in 1790, 1802, and 1805. As invading American settlers ruined the hunting grounds, the Lower Creek were forced to adopt the American, agricultural lifestyle and had forsaken many of their traditions. The younger men from the Upper Creek villages had been agitating for a return to traditional cultural and spiritual lifestyles, and Tenskwatawa's purification movement appealed to these village leaders and was heavily influential in their decisions to resist. Their response eventually blossomed into the Creek War or Red Stick War during 1813 and 1814.

Although it was reported that Tecumseh was banging the drums of war in October 1811, another reported speech he gave on his return to Tippecanoe struck a different tone. According to John Dunn Hunter, a white man who had been raised among the Osages after his parents were killed by the Kickapoos, reported that Tecumseh gave the following speech to the Osages: "Brothers, we all belong to one family; we are all children of the Great Spirit; we walk in the same path; slake our thirst at the same spring; and now affairs of the greatest concern lead us to smoke the pipe around the same council fire! Brothers, we are friends; we must assist each other to bear our burdens. The blood of many of our fathers and brothers has run like water on the ground, to satisfy the avarice of the white men. We, ourselves, are threatened with a great evil; nothing will pacify them but the destruction of all the red men. Brothers, when the white men first set foot on our grounds, they were hungry; they had no place on which to spread their blankets, or to kindle their fires."

"They were feeble; they could do nothing for themselves. Our fathers commiserated their distress, and shared freely with them whatever the Great Spirit had given his red children. They gave them food when hungry, medicine when sick, spread skins for them to sleep on, and gave them grounds, that they might hunt and raise corn. Brothers, the white people are like poisonous serpents: when chilled, they are feeble and harmless; but invigorate them with warmth, and they sting their benefactors to death. The white people came among us feeble; and now that we have made them strong, they wish to kill us, or drive us back, as they would wolves and panthers. Brothers, the white men are not friends to the Indians: at first, they only asked for land sufficient for a wigwam; now, nothing will satisfy them but the whole of our hunting grounds, from the rising to the setting sun. Brothers, the white men want more than our hunting grounds; they wish to kill our old men, women, and little ones. Brothers, many winters ago there was no land; the sun did not rise and set; all was darkness. The Great Spirit made all things. He gave the white people a home beyond the great waters. He supplied these grounds with game, and gave them to his red children; and he gave them strength and courage to defend them. Brothers, my people wish for peace; the red men all wish for peace; but where the white people are, there is no peace for them, except it be on the bosom of our mother. Brothers, the white men despise and cheat the

Indians; they abuse and insult them; they do not think the red men sufficiently good to live. The red men have borne many and great injuries; they ought to suffer them no longer. My people will not; they are determined on vengeance; they have taken up the tomahawk; they will make it fat with blood; they will drink the blood of the white people. Brothers, my people are brave and numerous; but the white people are too strong for them alone. I wish you to take up the tomahawk with them. If we all unite, we will cause the rivers to stain the great waters with their blood. Brothers, if you do not unite with us, they will first destroy us, and then you will fall an easy prey to them. They have destroyed many nations of red men, because they were not united, because they were not friends to each other. Brothers, the white people send runners amongst us; they wish to make us enemies, that they may sweep over and desolate our hunting grounds, like devastating winds, or rushing waters. Brothers, our Great Father over the great waters is angry with the white people, our enemies. He will send his brave warriors against them; he will send us rifles, and whatever else we want—he is our friend, and we are his children. Brothers, who are the white people that we should fear them? They cannot run fast, and are good marks to shoot at: they are only men; our fathers have killed many of them: we are not squaws, and we will stain the earth red with their blood. Brothers, the Great Spirit is angry with our enemies; he speaks in thunder, and the earth swallows up villages, and drinks up the Mississippi. The great waters will cover their lowlands; their corn cannot grow; and the Great Spirit will sweep those who escape to the hills from the earth with his terrible breath. Brothers, we must be united; we must smoke the same pipe; we must fight each other's battles; and, more than all, we must love the Great Spirit: he is for us; he will destroy our enemies, and make all his red children happy."

While Tecumseh was traveling, Tenskwatawa was left in charge of the Prophetstown settlement and the Confederacy, and in Tecumseh's absence the U.S. government had become increasingly concerned about the Prophetstown settlement and eventually endeavored to deal with the Native Americans there. An 1807 treaty between the Americans and members of the Sauk and Fox tribes left members of these tribes disaffected, and many of these angry warriors moved to Prophetstown and began imbibing the Prophet's teachings, swelling the ranks of the confederacy's warriors. The increasing popularity of Tenskwatawa's religious movement attracted these warriors with nothing left to lose and began to pose a real impediment to further settlement by Americans. Prior to traveling south to meet other Native American leaders, Tecumseh had likely made it clear to Tenskwatawa that he was as yet unready to openly challenge the United States and advised his brother not to make any provocative movements towards the Americans.

While this was going on, Governor Harrison had left the territory and put his secretary, John Gibson, in charge as acting Governor. Gibson had lived among the Native Americans in the area for many years and learned of Tecumseh's plans to travel south and recruit additional Native American allies for his confederacy and his desire to oppose further white encroachment onto tribal lands. By mid-September, Gibson had gathered militia troops and had sent urgent requests that Harrison return from Kentucky, so the Governor returned with a small detachment of regular

U.S. Army troops and assumed command of the mixed force.

After consulting with the Secretary of War in Washington, Governor Harrison decided that a show of military force was needed. Word had come to him that Tecumseh was away and would not be back for some time, so this seemed liked a good opportunity, he told Secretary Eustis, for breaking up the Indian confederacy. The original plan Harrison proposed was to go with a sufficiently-sized force, which the Indians would not feel they were able to attack, to the top of the new purchase of land under the Treaty of Fort Wayne and to build a fort there. This would show that the land was now irrevocably under U.S. control. If that show of force was not effective in dispersing the Prophet's party by demonstrating to them that the Prophet was unable to defend them, Harrison proposed proceeding farther northward to Prophetstown itself in order to seize some hostages to enforce compliance with his demands.

In early September, to foster splits among the Indians living on the Wabash preparatory to his march, Harrison called together a council with the Miamis and their allies at Fort Wayne. Addressing them as "my children," Harrison told them that he discerned a dark cloud on the Wabash but that this would bring danger only to the Indians, not to himself. The followers of the Prophet were to be deemed hostile Indians, and for their own safety, other Indians were commanded to break with them and to inform on their movements, as they were required to do under the terms of the Treaty of Greenville the Indians had signed with the U.S. in 1795. The Miami chief Little Turtle was compliant, but the Wea chief Laprusiuer was not.

By this time, Harrison was already putting together an expeditionary force. This consisted of eight companies of Army soldiers from the 4th U.S. Infantry Regiment, one company from the Riflemen Regiment under Col. John P. Boyd from Philadelphia, three troops of light dragoons, and Kentucky and Indiana militia members in their buckskins shirts and carrying scalping knives and tomahawks. The total force numbered altogether somewhere between 1,000-1,200 men according to various estimates, and on the morning of September 26th, they started northward from Fort Knox near Vincennes with Harrison in command and all their heavy baggage on boats.

**A replica of the palisade wall around Fort Knox**

Crossing a level, open prairie lying near the river banks, they reached the present-day site of Terre Haute, Indiana, 60 miles up the Wabash River, on October 3rd. There, overlooking the Wabash on the east side in a grove of trees and just a couple of miles south from a Wea Indian village, they erected a fort named "Fort Harrison." The fort's construction took most of the month. With the flour ration going short after several weeks and no resupply yet because the merchants had been shot at on the river, the soldiers helped feed themselves with catfish and venison procured from the land. Militia members who knew how to forage found bee trees for the sweet honey, but some militiamen still deserted.

Harrison construed some small probes by Indians on their camp as signs that a full-scale war with the Indians had begun, so he sent to Kentucky for reinforcements. He dispatched some Delawares who had come to the camp with a message to Prophetstown, which was basically an ultimatum calling on all the non-Shawnees to depart from there and go back to where they came from. The Delawares reported to him that their mission had been met with scorn and derision; Harrison was clearly not succeeding in his mission of instilling respect and fear into the breasts of the defiant Indians. Thus, he concluded that he needed to march his force 80 miles onward to Prophetstown itself to make a heavier impression on them.

More provisions and some reinforcements arrived, but Harrison did not order his forces to march on Prophetstown until he had received a letter from Secretary of War Eustis that he took as providing him with the authorization to do so. At the same time, this letter suggested that hostilities be avoided if possible in the course of insisting on the fulfillment of the treaty's stipulations. Leaving behind some men to garrison the new fort, along with those men unfit for duty, the expeditionary force – now with 880 soldiers – resumed its advance northward on October 29th. Near the mouth of the Vermillion River, the expedition stopped again for two days to build a blockhouse, and the expedition's boats and surplus baggage were left there under guard.

Arriving near Prophetstown late in the day of November 6th, Harrison ordered his forces into their battle formation. Prophetstown, although not fully ready, had been fortified; the Native American camp was surrounded by a massive zigzag log wall with port-holes cut at regular intervals for shooting out of, behind which were trenches for the warriors to sit in. As Harrison's soldiers came within sight, the Indians, fearing that an attack was imminent, scrambled to get behind their breastworks.

Three Indians on horseback carrying a white flag came out to parley, and after consulting for a short time with Harrison, they galloped back to the village. The soldiers continued their march to within 150 yards of the village, at which point more consultations with the Indians transpired. Harrison, although urged by some of his officers to attack them forthwith, agreed to meet with Tenskwatawa the following day.

Tired from their long day's march and not expecting an attack, Harrison did not order the camp to be fortified by felling trees, as was the customary practice, but the force encamped in a defensive rectangle (or parallelogram) and spent the night with their guns loaded and close at hand. On the western side of Harrison's perimeter, a small creek (Burnet Creek) ran, providing a natural impediment to an attack, and a very steep bluff on the eastern side precluded any attack from that direction. Only the narrow southern point of Harrison's perimeter and the northeastern side, southwest of a Catholic mission, posed serious threats of attack.

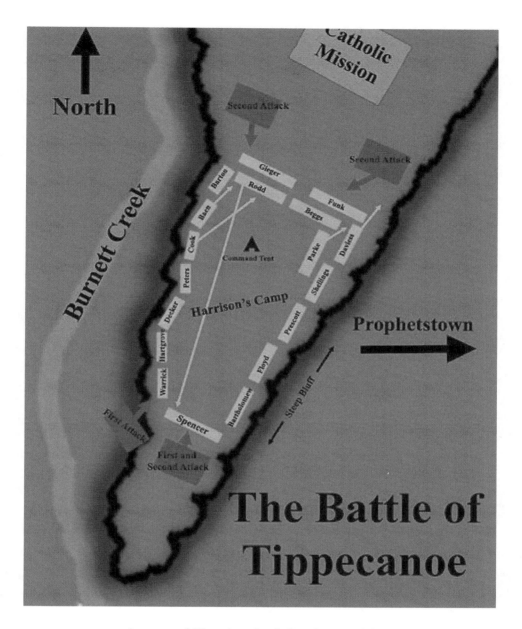

**A map of Harrison's defensive position**

Sentinels were posted that night, and the Yellow Jackets, led by Captain Spier Spencer, manned the southern point of the perimeter. After setting sentinels, Harrison and his officers and men retired. It was a cold night with drizzly rain, and at 4:00 a.m. that morning, November 7, just as the camp began to awaken and would soon be lining up in formation to start the day, the Indians attacked with loud, terrifying war whoops. Coming out of the woods, the natives were able to break into one side of the hollow rectangle as the warriors rushed in among the Yellow Jackets manning the southern sector of the perimeter. The Yellow Jackets' captain, Spier Spencer, was among the first casualties. Though wounded in the head, the Yellow Jackets' leader urged his men to fight, and Spencer managed to make it to his feet after being wounded only to be shot through both legs and fall again. Continuing to encourage his company, Spencer was raised to his feet by other soldiers, but he was then shot through the torso and immediately died. Harrison would later inform officials in Washington, "Spencer was wounded in the head. He exhorted his men to fight valiantly. He was shot through both thighs and fell; still continuing to encourage them, he was raised up, and received [another] ball through his body, which put an immediate end to his existence."

Spencer was briefly replaced by his two surviving company officers, but they too were soon wounded and killed. Leaderless, the Yellow Jackets began to fall back with the retreating sentries, toward the center of the perimeter. Two companies of reserve troops, roused by the sound of battle, relieved the retreating militiamen by reforming a line and turning the Native American attack. The perimeter was reformed and again manned, but a second charge targeted both the northern and southern sides simultaneously. Once inside the rectangle, the Indians briefly held the advantage since the white soldiers did not want to fire into the darkness for fear of hitting their own men. The white soldiers were also silhouetted against the fires they had built and kept going overnight to dry out their clothing and gear.

In the frenzied early moments of the battle, Harrison's servant could not locate Harrison's usual grey mare, so Harrison mounted a darker horse to ride to rally his troops. This was a fortuitous accident for him because the natives knew he rode a light-colored horse and were looking for him on it. Another officer who was with a white horse was shot dead early on. Harrison did receive a shot through the brim of his hat but remained otherwise unscathed.

All told, the Indians made four or five fierce charges on the camp, which they coordinated by blowing on a whistle, but each time they were driven back. As the dawn brought daylight, the advantage shifted to the white soldiers, who were now able to charge in formation, and their mounted men were able cut down the fleeing Indians. After about two hours of strenuous fighting, the battle came to an end. Among the whites, 188 officers and men were killed and wounded, a fairly serious loss. The bodies of 38 Indians were found on the field, and several more were discovered later in or around Prophetstown.

With a rumor circulating that Tecumseh was on the way with another 1,000 warriors, Harrison's men spent the rest of the day fortifying their camp, but no more attacks were forthcoming. Tecumseh was not present for the Battle of Tippecanoe or located anywhere nearby; along with a hand-picked delegation of six Shawnees, six Kickapoos and six Potawatomis, the Shawnee leader was still on an extended six-month trip through the South visiting with the Creeks, Choctaws, Cherokees and other tribes to try to gain their support for his plan of a greater pan-Indian confederacy. On his way back north, Tecumseh also visited tribes in Missouri where he was present for the great earthquakes. According to some accounts, when he returned to Indiana in January 1812, he was exceedingly angry with his brother for having launched a war before he felt their plans were sufficiently matured.

As Harrison's men soon discovered, far from getting ready to attack again, the natives had precipitously abandoned Prophetstown and left behind all kinds of supplies in the form of corn, hogs, poultry, numerous brass cooking kettles. A few guns, some of which were apparently gifts from the British, were still in their original coverings and had never been used. The herd of cattle brought along by the soldiers for meat had been driven off by the Indians, so the soldiers had to subsist on horse meat or whatever they were able to plunder from the village. Harrison had his men burn the town and its contents and then marched his troops back to Vincennes, stopping at the blockhouse on the Vermillion River to put his wounded men into canoes. From his headquarters near Prophetstown on November 8th, Harrison had already sent a dispatch to the Secretary of War claiming the battle was a "complete and decisive victory."

A number of the white soldiers who participated in the Battle of Tippecanoe kept journals or later left reminiscences. Charles Larrabee, a lieutenant in the 4th Regiment, wrote a series of informative letters before and after the battle to a cousin in Connecticut, and before the battle, he had expressed hopes that the situation would terminate without bloodshed. Judge Isaac Naylor, at that time sergeant of an Indiana militia riflemen company, recalled how a friend and fellow soldier had told him of a bad dream that he believed "foreboded something fatal to him or to some of his family." His friend was shot by an Indian and fell dead in the mass confusion at the commencement of the attack. Naylor also described how nearly all the dead Indians left on the battlefield were scalped and had their scalps mounted on the militia's muskets, which he considered a barbarous practice but excusable under the circumstances.

Conversely, a different report on the nature of the battle reached British ears at Amherstburg in Upper Canada (Ontario) via a Kickapoo chief who was in the action. He claimed that the attack had been launched to avenge two young Winnebagos who, out of curiosity, had approached the American encampment overnight and had been shot at by the white pickets. Pretending to be wounded, they had jumped up and tomahawked the soldiers who had come to dispatch them. According to this report, only about 100 warriors, consisting of Winnebagos and Kickapoos, were involved directly in the fighting, and they drove the whites back and forth between them until they ran out of arrows and ammunition. Furthermore, the Kickapoo asserted that while Harrison had been able to destroy a lot of the village's corn, other corn had survived concealed underground. The British officer wrote to his superior, "The Prophet and his people do not appear as a vanquished enemy; they re-occupy their former ground."

Years after what became known as the Battle of Tippecanoe, Tenskwatawa told Lewis Cass, the Governor of the Michigan Territory, that he had not ordered the attack that started the battle. Instead, he accused the Winnebagos in his camp of starting the attack. Other accounts corroborate this, but some claim that the evening before the attack Tenskwatawa spurred the attack by claiming to have consulted with spirits and instructing a small band to try to murder Harrison in his tent to avoid the impending battle. According to this account, Tenskwatawa had assured the attacking warriors that he would cast spells preventing them from being harmed or killed, but when that obviously didn't happen, they were enraged.

The Miami chief Little Eyes reported to Harrison a description of the events that may have been tailored to what he thought Harrison would want to hear. Little Eyes was near Prophetstown looking to meet with Harrison when the fighting took place, and he described Tenskwatawa as having been the architect of the attack. Little Chief further claimed the Prophet was being blamed for the failure of his protective charms and was thus being treated as a pariah by his former followers. According to this report, a crestfallen Tenskwatawa had tried to shift blame onto his wife, whom he said he did not know had been menstruating at the time. His wife had touched the bowl containing his sacred beans and deer hoofs, and for that reason he pled to be given a second chance.

### The War of 1812

Roughly one month after the Battle of Tippecanoe and the destruction of Prophetstown, a series of severe earthquakes struck the region on December 11, 1811, centered on the Mississippi River town New Madrid, located in present-day Missouri. This was interpreted as the natural world once again speaking to the Native Americans, and their leaders assumed that Tenskwatawa's apocalyptic predictions were coming to pass. Tecumseh's confederacy gained even greater support, and violent opposition to white settlement grew more frequent after the Battle of Tippecanoe; settlers in isolated areas throughout the Indiana and Illinois region were targeted, and many were killed. This renewed violence and the rebuilding of Prophetstown attracted the attention of the Territorial authorities, and a campaign mounted by the U.S. military during 1812 again destroyed a partially rebuilt but deserted Prophetstown.

By June of 1812, Tecumseh's Confederacy was at least as strong as it had been before the Battle of Tippecanoe, and on June 18 Tecumseh announced that he intended to travel to Fort Malden (a British fort in northwestern Ohio) to gather lead and powder, not knowing that the British and United States were already at war. Prior to actual declaration of war, President James Madison began to marshal his forces in an attempt to defend the Northwest region (present-day Ohio, Indiana, and Michigan), and then Secretary of War William Eustis appointed William Hull, the Governor of the Michigan Territory, to oversee the defensive operations. The region had few military assets (very few regular Army troops were in the area), and in response, Madison ordered that an army be formed and moved quickly to the vital frontier outpost at Detroit.

**William Hull**

Hull initially refused to assume command of the newly formed army, but he eventually agreed and moved south to Dayton, Ohio, to lead a force of three regiments of Ohio militia in late May. The regiments under Hull began moving north towards Detroit, but it was very slow going, and the column was joined en route by the 4th Infantry Regiment, under Lieutenant Colonel James Miller. While moving through the Black Swamp (in present-day northwestern Ohio), a courier reached Hull with a dispatch from Eustis dated June 18 (he received it on June 26), urging Hull to rush to Detroit because war was looming. A second letter, also dated June 18, stated that war had been declared, however, because it was sent by regular mail, it did not reach Hull until July 2.

At the time, Hull and his troops were at the Maumee River in Ohio, and in an attempt to speed his movement to Detroit Hull decided to hire the schooner *Cuyahoga* to carry his dispatches, personal mail, medical supplies, and sick troops. Unfortunately, the British forces in the area knew that the two nations were already at war, and the *Cuyahoga* was captured by the *HMS General Hunter* the following day. Hull and his column eventually arrived at Detroit on July 5, 1812, where he was reinforced by 140 Michigan militiamen. Despite being short on food and supplies, Eustis ordered Hull to advance on Fort Malden, but the commander was hampered by the refusal of some militiamen to serve outside of the United States and the news of British attacks elsewhere.

The British had been frustrated by their previous efforts to form alliances with Native

American peoples, due largely in part to the different ways they fought. European armies had always preferred fighting in open fields, operating under the assumption that their foot soldiers could suffer large numbers of casualties without affecting the existence of the standing unit. After all, there were always more conscripts to fill the levies required by the military. Conversely, Native Americans societies could not suffer such horrendous losses, and their tribes' livelihoods were based on the survival of sufficient numbers of young men being able to hunt and defend the tribe against enemies. As a result, each warrior made his own survival decisions in combat. Additionally, the British could not understand the Native Americans' tendency to rely on omens, signs, and visions to determine their action in battle.

For these reasons, Tecumseh was an appealing leader to the British commanders. He never relied on supernatural influences to make combat decisions, and he operated in combat as though he was a formally trained soldier, having been engaged in combat operations for nearly 20 years. The first appearance of Tecumseh during the War of 1812 occurred at a war council held at Sandwich (Windsor), Ontario, on July 7, 1812, where he is described as having played "a conspicuous part."

Moving slowly towards Fort Malden, Hull and his column captured Sandwich on July 13, and, encouraged by the apparent neutrality of Native Americans he encountered and the desertion of some Canadian militiamen, he continued his thrust into British territory, sending probing detachments farther and farther into enemy territory. On July 17, Tecumseh participated in an attack on the American garrison at Fort Mackinac, where a force of Native Americans and Canadians surprised the American defenders, an incident that began to convince Hull that there were numerous hostile Native Americans in the region. The American commander grew fearful that his forces might be cut off from supplies that at the time arrived via a circuitous route that ran through northwestern Ohio.

On August 5, 1812, his fears were realized. Tecumseh and other Native American leaders ambushed a supply train bound for Hull's troops near present-day Trenton, Michigan on that day, and combined with news that British troops were advancing from the Niagara River area this was enough to convince Hull to withdraw his troops from Canadian territory on August 8. On August 9, Tecumseh and Roundhead (another Native American leader) led a group of Native Americans who joined some British regulars and some Canadian militiamen in a bloody attack on an American force south of Detroit that had been sent to protect a supply train en route to Hull's command.

Around this time, Tecumseh met Isaac Brock, a British officer for whom he developed an instant affinity, and in turn the British officer would eventually become a believer in Tecumseh's vision for a Native American state south of the Great Lakes. Brock would say of Tecumseh, "I found some extraordinary characters. He who attracted most my attention was a Shawnee chief, Tecumset, brother to the Prophet, who for the last two years has carried on contrary to our remonstrances an active warfare against the United States. A more sagacious or more gallant warrior does not, I believe, exist. He was the admiration of every one who conversed with him."

**Brock**

Brock was the regional British commander, and he reached Fort Malden at the head of reinforcements on August 13. He immediately proposed a daring attack on Fort Detroit which greatly pleased Tecumseh and the Native American forces (about 600 warriors), who had been concerned at the traditional British caution during infantry engagements. The British commander sent a letter to Hull stating that he had no intention of exterminating the Americans but would likely be unable to control the Native American troops serving with him from the moment the battle began.

In reality, the letter was merely the first part of a series of deceptions designed to assure the British victory with minimum casualties. On August 15, Brock ordered a bombardment of Fort Detroit, and the following day the British and Native American forces crossed the river hoping to cut supply lines and lay siege to the fort. In response to the attack and movement, Hull dispatched 400 men under Lieutenant Colonels MacArthur and Cass to open the southern supply route. To avoid being pinned between this force and the fort, Brock turned his column to the west and planned to attack from that direction. Meanwhile, Tecumseh led his forces through gaps in the woods, issuing war cries and giving the Americans the impression that the Native American force was far larger than it actually was.

The deceptions continued as Brock had extra uniforms from his 41st Regiment distributed to Canadian militiamen to make it appear that he had more regular troops. He also told his soldiers to light individual fires, greatly multiplying the apparent size of his forces. Troops were ordered to march about, giving the impression that large numbers of soldiers were being positioned for an assault.

During the continued bombardment, a ball struck the officer mess within the fort and caused several casualties. For the American commander, the cannon strike was the final straw; he broke down. Fearing annihilation at the hands of Tecumseh's warriors, Hull ordered a white flag raised and began surrender negotiations. The Americans holding Fort Detroit lost seven men killed and about 2,500 captured. The 400-man force that had left the fort was also surrendered, as was an approaching supply train. The combined British/Native American force suffered two soldiers wounded, and the victory, won by guile and deceit, radically changed the military situation in the Northwest, dashing American hopes of an easy march through Canada's back door. According to legend, Brock and Tecumseh rode into Detroit side by side and the British commander gave the Native American a gift of a sash as a mark of respect. Brock was hailed as the Hero of Upper Canada, but his status would be short-lived when he was killed a couple of months later at the victorious Battle of Queenston Heights.

Tecumseh would not live much longer than his new friend. Tecumseh largely disappears from the records during the winter of 1812-1813, and some sources indicate that he may have spent much of the time recuperating from some unnamed illness. Other sources claim he again traveled south in a second attempt to win support for his confederacy from southern tribes.

In April of 1813, Tecumseh reappears in the record, and he and Roundhead are described as leading a force of some 1,200 Native American warriors, who together with 900 British regulars under Major General Henry Procter laid siege to Fort Meigs (near present-day Perrysburg, Ohio). The American defenders held off the attacking British/Native American attack, but a column of reinforcements bound for the fort was attacked and 500 men were taken captives. These unfortunate souls were carried off by the Native Americans and executed by fire, a common method of killing enemies among Algonquin tribes. Procter did not interfere in the murder, and it only ended when Tecumseh arrived on the scene and ordered an end to the carnage. It was this type of action that built respect among whites for Tecumseh and likely explains why even those he opposed held him in such high regard. A second attack on the fort was attempted in July, but the British committed only a small number of regulars to the attack and lacked proper equipment, leading to the abandonment of the plan.

By this time, several other Native American leaders had joined forces with Tecumseh, swelling the ranks of warriors to about 3,000. Procter turned his sights on Fort Stephenson (present-day Fremont, Ohio), but the defenders there also put up a stiff resistance and repelled the attackers. Increasingly demoralized by heavy casualties taken at Fort Stephenson, the mood of the British and Native American troops only worsened with the defeat of the British Navy at the Battle of Put-In Bay (Ohio) in early September. The 4,000 troops under Procter (1,000 British regulars and 3,000 warriors), now had no way of obtaining resupply, and their commander knew that General William Henry Harrison was preparing an invasion of the Detroit frontier.

Without consulting his indigenous allies, Procter order the dismantling of Fort Malden and planned to make for the head of Lake Ontario in hopes of escaping to British territory. Tecumseh, suspecting the British would depart without opposing the Americans, begged Procter to arm his warriors so they could attempt to defend their homeland alone. In return, Procter promised to stop at the fork of the Thames River and turn to face the approaching Americans. Agreeing to these terms, Tecumseh and some of the Native American warriors agreed to join the British retreat.

During the retreat, Tecumseh constantly harangued Procter, urging him to turn and face the Americans. At one point Tecumseh reportedly told Procter, "Father, listen!—The Americans have not yet defeated us by land—neither are we sure that they have done so by water—we therefore wish to remain here, and fight our enemy, should they make their appearance... Father!—You have got the arms and the ammunition which our great father sent for his red children. If you have an idea of going away, give them to us. Our lives are in the hands of the Great Spirit. We are determined to defend our lands, and if it be his will, we wish to leave our bones upon them."

When the agreed upon point of defense was reached – the fork of the Thames River – Procter continued ahead of the column, refusing to stop and allegedly looking for a more advantageous position. Numerous Native American warriors, now thinking no defense would be made, abruptly left the column. Tecumseh was reportedly livid.

By early October, the Americans were catching up with the retreating British/Native American column, and Tecumseh led a delaying action that attacked the approaching American force, hoping to delay them. A small ship carrying supplies for the retreating troops ran aground about the same time and was captured by American troops. The retreating column had been placed on half rations during their flight from Fort Malden, and the men were already starving and exhausted.

Procter finally found the ground he wished to defend and turned to face the Americans on October 5,1813 at Moraviantown. As the Americans approached, the highly demoralized British troops formed battle lines, and the remaining Native American warriors led by Tecumseh were formed in a swampy area on the British right in position to provide flanking fire against the Americans. The initial American attack, a cavalry charge by mounted Kentucky volunteers, broke through the British lines, and the British immediately turned and fled from the field. A group of about twenty irregular cavalrymen then turned and charged into Tecumseh's position, hoping to draw attention away from the main American attack. Tecumseh and his men stood their ground and with determined volley fire stopped the charge.

The horse-borne troops were bogged down by the muddy ground, and it's believed that Tecumseh was killed during this engagement. Not surprisingly, different accounts of Tecumseh's death have been given. One member of the Ottawa later claimed that Tecumseh was severely wounded by a musket ball but continued defiantly fighting, stating, "One of my legs is shot off! But leave me one or two guns loaded — I am going to have a last shot. Be quick and go!" Another account claimed that he was killed by a pistol shot while attacking Colonel Richard M. Johnson of Kentucky with a tomahawk, but that has since been discounted by historians.

However it happened, the rapid convergence of American reinforcements and the quickly spreading news of Tecumseh's death broke the Native American resistance. The British/Native American defeat at the Battle of Moraviantown (usually called the Battle of the Thames) effectively restored American control over the Northwest frontier, and despite a few skirmishes later in the war, no other real battles occurred in the theater.

**Depiction of Tecumseh's death at the Battle of the Thames**

After the battle, Native American warriors supposedly recovered Tecumseh's body from the battlefield. Rumors held that his bones had no permanent resting place and were repeatedly moved. According to common knowledge they are lost to history, but in 1931 a group of Canadian ex-servicemen who had served with Native American troops during World War I held a grand council and declared that a set of human remains that had been preserved on Walpole

Island were those of Tecumseh. The local Soldiers' Club raised money to erect a monument over the burial site of the Native American leader's remains.

It's safe to say the most significant event of the Battle of Moraviantown was the death of Tecumseh, and Roundhead was also killed, depriving the Native Americans of leadership. Tenskwatawa was present at the battle, but he fled with British troops after the fighting started. The confederacy Tecumseh had struggled to build died with him, and his death marked the end of organized resistance to white settlement among Native American groups east of the Mississippi River.

Perhaps the truest mark of Tecumseh's character is that he was admired even by his most ardent foes. William Henry Harrison would later state of the Indian leader, "If it were not for the vicinity of the United States, he would perhaps be the founder of an empire that would rival in glory Mexico or Peru. No difficulties deter him. For four years he has been in constant motion. You see him today on the Wabash, and in a short time hear of him on the shores of Lake Erie or Michigan, or on the banks of the Mississippi, and wherever he goes he makes an impression favorable to his purpose." As Tecumseh's biographer Devin Bent aptly put it, "It is difficult to feel greatness after a lapse of 200 years, but Tecumseh truly seems admirable. He was noble in his speech and behavior, adamant in his opposition to U.S. expansion, farsighted in his policies, brave in battle, yet merciful and protective toward captives."

If the name of one of America's most famous generals is any indication, Tecumseh was almost immediately viewed positively among his American contemporaries, despite his resistance. In 1820, less than a decade removed from Tecumseh's death, a young boy would be born in Lancaster, Ohio and named Tecumseh Sherman. The boy, who would eventually grow up to become a legendary Civil War general, William Tecumseh Sherman, explained that his father named him Tecumseh because he had "caught a fancy for the great chief of the Shawnees." Somewhat ironically, the nation Tecumseh fought so bitterly against would commemorate him in countless ways, including naming everything from townships to battleships after him.

### The End of the Prophet

Historians have claimed that the prediction of invulnerability at Tippecanoe destroyed Tenskwatawa's credibility, immediately ending his influence, but that seems to be overstated and could even be fiction. Prophetstown's population at the point of its destruction is unknown, but its residents scattered before and during the battle. The town's women and children probably began evacuating the night before the battle. Some of the non-Shawnee residents seem to have returned to their home tribes, some retreated into the remaining forested regions, some sought refuge with tribes still at peace, like the Miamis, and some found refuge under British protection. Some began to rebuild.

In fact, it appears that the Prophet was able to retain a fairly strong spiritual following until after the War of 1812. Prophetstown was rebuilt, and the massive pair of earthquakes that struck on December 16, 1811 with their epicenter near New Madrid in present-day Arkansas convinced some Indians (and also some whites) that they were living in an apocalyptic time period. This benefitted Tenskwatawa, as it appeared to be a fulfillment of his prophecies. A newspaper reported that a fortunate Indian who had been swallowed up by the earth but disgorged declared "the Shawnee Prophet has caused the earthquake to destroy the whites." Whether Tenskwatawa made that claim for himself was not recorded, but a legend persisted that Tecumseh had told doubters among the Creeks during his visit to the South that the earth would soon tremble and they would regret not listening to him.

After the death of Tecumseh, the Prophet became the leader of the Shawnee in Canada, but his leadership in war was a pale imitation of his brother's. The British tried to get him to lead war parties, but he declined, until finally agreeing to lead one to the Niagara frontier. His small force reached a battlefield on July 6, 1815, not long after the Battle of Chippewa had ended with an American victory on the Canadian side of the Niagara. The cautious Prophet decided to withdraw before any more fighting occurred, and when he left, most of the other natives with the British also decided to leave. The British would have retreated anyway, but they were weakened by the departure of the warriors (Edmunds "Tenskwatawa").

The Battle of the Thames and the several battles following it were not major American victories, but they were enough to end native resistance in most of the Old Northwest and represented the final attempts at a pan-Indian confederacy east of the Mississippi. The fighting also essentially ended the border conflict across the Great Lakes between America and Canada, which meant the tribes on the American side of the border no longer had reliable foreign allies.

The Shawnee in the Wapakoneta settlements in northwest Ohio sided with the United States, and hoped that their friendliness would allow them to continue living where they were. The state of Ohio was experiencing explosive growth, from 230,000 in 1810 to 580,000 in 1820. Even though the Wapakoneta settlement was in a swampy, difficult area, settlers wanted access to that land, and the pressure for the cession of the remaining Indian lands in all of the Old Northwest Territory was relentless. Migrants flooded in, Indiana became a state in 1816, and Michigan became a state in 1818. The settlers coming in after the war of 1813 were apparently somewhat different than many of the earlier settlers. Settlers migrating into Indiana before 1813 tended to be experienced in fighting, and many tended to keep moving from one place to another as the frontier moved ever westward (Edmunds "Justice" 49).

These later settlers did not consider the tribal peoples to be a mortal danger. Natives were instead viewed as a nuisance who occupied land that could be better used by white farmers. Settlers were interested in establishing family farms and forming communities, replicating conditions in older settled areas to the east (Edmunds "Justice" 49).

In 1817, government negotiators met with the Wapakoneta Shawnees and discussed matters of land rights. The government wanted the Shawnee to settle on farms and surrender any land remaining after allotting the land to individual families. The Shawnee wanted small reservations for Wapakoneta, Lewiston, and Hog Creek settlements. A treaty was agreed on, but it was rejected by Congress in 1818 (Lakomaki 620-21).

The Prophet remained in Canada after the end of the War of 1812. Tenskwatawa was interested in returning to the United States, but only if he could return to the Tippecanoe and Wabash area. In 1816, he met with Michigan Governor Lewis Cass and found out that he would not be allowed to return to the Wabash, so he returned to Canada. His remaining supporters, about two dozen families, settled in a place called Cedar Creek, where they stayed for the next eight years. They existed on rations and supplies reluctantly supplied by the British, leaving them impoverished. All the while, the once influential Prophet had a quarrelsome relationship with the British Indian agents (Edmunds "Tenskwatawa").

In 1825, federal authorities invited Tenskwatawa back into the United States from his exile in Upper Canada (now called Ontario). They decided he was no longer a threat, and he was invited in the hope that he could persuade the Wapakoneta Shawnee to leave Ohio. The Prophet accepted the offer, and he subsequently persuaded about 250 of the remaining Wapakoneta Shawnee to accompany him west to the land designated for a reservation in Kansas. It took them more than a year to arrive. The remaining Wapakoneta Shawnee faced ever-increasing pressure, and, finally in 1831, they gave in, exchanging their remaining Ohio land for land on the reservation in Kansas (Lakomaki 621-23).

Battling the Shawnee ended up contributing enormously to the political success of two American soldiers. The Kentuckian who killed Tecumseh, Richard M. Johnson, was elected Vice President in 1836, and the successful Van Buren campaign boasted that Johnson killed Tecumseh. Ironically, they were defeated in the 1840 election by William Henry Harrison, whose campaign famously used the slogan "Tippecanoe and Tyler too." As that suggests, Harrison's supporters transformed the Battle of Tippecanoe from a bloody and inconclusive skirmish into a major victory. The campaign published illustrations showing Harrison on horseback fighting the natives, looking more like Napoleon than a frontier general with a backwoods army in the wilderness.

Today, Harrison's presidency is best known for being the shortest. It lasted only 31 days because he got sick, possibly on Inauguration Day. Tyler, who assumed the presidency from 1841-1845, is perhaps best known for having 15 children.

By the time Tenskwatawa led the 250 Wapakoneta Shawnee to their reservation in eastern Kansas, few of them considered him to be anything more than a leader and Tecumseh's brother. He had a few remaining followers, but he lived out a quiet life with whatever was left of them on the reservation.

So far as is known, he had no more trances with new revelations from the Creator, perhaps because he apparently abstained from alcohol during his later years. One of the most notable events in his life during this stage was that he posed for a painting by renowned artist George Catlin in 1832, and the painting has defined the image of Tenskwatawa ever since.

The Prophet died peacefully on the reservation in 1836, having managed to survive so many of his people's battles.

## Online Resources

Other books about Native American history by Charles River Editors

## Further Reading

Adams, Paul. "Colonel Henry Bouquet's Ohio Expedition of 1764." *Pennsylvania History* 40 (2), April 1973. 138-147.

Buffenbarger, Thomas. "St. Clair's Defeat in 1791: A Defeat in the Wilderness That Helped Forge Today's U.S. Army. Army Heritage and Education Center, 2011. army.mil/articles/65594/st-clairs-campaign-of-1791/. Accessed November 24, 2021.

Bilodeaux, Christopher. "Creating an Enemy in the Borderlands: King Philip's War in Maine, 1675-78." *Maine History* 41 (1), 2013. 10-41.

Britannica. "Second Seminole War." britannica.com/event/Second-Seminole-War/. Accessed November 16, 2021.

British Battles.com. "Battle of Monongahela 1755." britishbattles.com/french-indian-war/battle-of-monongahela-1755. Accessed November 15, 2021.

Brown, Michael. "Death in the Land of Flowers: Environment as Enemy in the Second Seminole War." Thesis, University of Central Florida, 2020. USF Electronic Theses and Dissertations, 2020. Accessed November 16, 2021.

Brummel, Steve. "'A Service Truly Critical' : The British Army and Warfare With the North American Indians 1751-1764." *War in History* 5 (2), April 1998. 156-175.

Cassell, Frank. "The Braddock Expedition of 1755: Catastrophe in the Wilderness." *Pennsylvania Legacies* 5 (1), May 2005. 11-15.

Fern, Elizabeth. "Biological Warfare in Eighteenth Century North America: Beyond Jeffrey Amherst." *Journal of American History* 80 (4), March 2000. 1552-1580.

Gasparro, Joseph. "'The Desired Effect' : Pontiac's Rebellion and the Native American

Struggle to Survive in Britain's North American Conquest." *The Gettysburg Journal* 6, 2007. 1-27.

Loxahatchee Battlefield Preservation. "Information About the Second Seminole War." trailsoffloridaindianheritage.com/Loxahatchee-river-park/. Accessed November 24, 2021.

Lyons, Chuck. "Braddock's Defeat, 1755, French and Indian War." History.net. historynet.com/Braddocks-defeat-1755-french-indian-war.htm/. Accessed November 15, 2021.

Maine History Online. "1668-1774, Settlement and Strife." mainememory.net/sitebuilder/site/897/page/1308/. Accessed November 15, 2021.

National Park Service. "Osceola." nps.gov/people/Osceola.htm/. Accessed November 16, 2020.

Neely, Sylvia. "Mason Locke Weems' 'Life of George Washington' and the Myth of Braddock's Defeat." Virginia Magazine of Biography and History 107 (1), Winter 1999. 45-72.

Noble, John. *King Philip's War in Maine, 1675-1678.* Thesis, University of Maine. Digital commons.library.omaine.edu/etd/. Accessed November 15, 2021.

O'Brien, Andy and Will Chapman. "Radial Mainers: A Brutal Race War Ends in Victory for the Abenaki." *Mainer*, February 11, 2020.

Scarlett, Daniel. "This Inglorious War: The Second Seminole War, the Ad Hoc Origins of American Imperialism, and the Silence of Slavery." Dissertation, Washington University of St. Louis, 2011. openscholarship.wusl.edu/c.cgigi/viewcontent?article/. Accessed November 15, 2021.

Stewart, Richard, et. al. *The United States Army and the Forging of a Nation 1775-1917.* Washington, D.C., 2009.

Taylor, Alan. "*American Revolutions, A Continental History.*" New York: W.W. Norton, 2016.

Taylor, Alan. "Pontiac's War." American Heritage, Winter 2010. americanheritage.com/ pontiacs-war/. Accessed November 15, 2021.

Treuer, Alan. "*The Indian Wars.*" Washington D.C.: National Geographic, 2016.

Warner, Michael. "General Josiah Harmar's Campaign Reconsidered: How the Americans Lost the Battle of Kekionga." *Indiana Magazine of History* 83 (1), Winter 1987. 43-64.

Zander, Cecily. "The Second Seminole War as a Civil War Training Ground." *Emerging Civil War*, June 4, 2020. emergingcivilwar.com/2020/06/04/the-second-seminole-war-as-a- civil-war-training-ground/. Accessed November 24, 2021.

Made in United States
Troutdale, OR
09/07/2024

22654788R00031